THE WAY OF THE SPIRIT

The
WAY
OF THE
SPIRIT

Using *the* Gifts,
Showing *the* Fruits

DAVID M. KNIGHT

TWENTY-THIRD
PUBLICATIONS
twentythirdpublications.com

Come, Holy Spirit, fill the hearts of your faithful.
And kindle in us the fire of your divine love.
Send forth your Spirit, Lord, and our hearts
    will be regenerated.
And you will renew the face of the earth!
God, by the light of the Holy Spirit,
you instruct the hearts of your faithful:

Grant us by the Gifts of Wisdom, Understanding,
    Knowledge, Counsel,
Family Spirit, Strength, and Awe of the Lord
that we may not be conformed to this world
but transformed by the renewal of our minds,
so that we might discern and do
what is good, acceptable, and pleasing to you,
    and perfect;

And so be the aroma of Christ in the world
through Love, Joy, Peace,
Patient Endurance, Kindness, Generosity,
Faithfulness, Gentleness, and the Self-Control
    of total surrender to your Spirit.

TWENTY-THIRD PUBLICATIONS
One Montauk Avenue, Suite 200
New London, CT 06320
(860) 437-3012 or (800) 321-0411
www.twentythirdpublications.com

ISBN: 978-1-62785-597-6
Printed in the U.S.A.

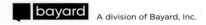

A division of Bayard, Inc.

Contents

Introduction

Why We Need This

"Be holy, because I am holy."
1 PETER 1:16

Pope Francis has written to "repropose the call to holiness in a practical way for our own time." He says, "The Lord has chosen each one of us 'to be holy and blameless before him in love' (Ephesians 1:4)....The Lord asks everything of us, and in return he offers us true life, the happiness for which we were created. He wants us to be saints and not to settle for a bland and mediocre existence" (*Rejoice and Be Glad*, 2, 1).

The first pope wrote: "As he who called you is holy, be holy yourselves in all your conduct; for it is written, 'You shall be holy, because I am holy'" (1 Peter 1:16).

The current pope writes: "Let the grace of your Baptism bear fruit in a path of holiness....Do not be dismayed, for the power of the Holy Spirit enables you to do this, and holiness, in the end, is the fruit of the Holy Spirit in your life" (see Galatians 5:22–23, *Rejoice and Be Glad*, 15).

Obviously, Christians should focus on experiencing the "fruit of the Holy Spirit," not just on living good human lives according to the Ten Commandments. To live only by the Ten Commandments is to live a sub-Christian life. Christians are called—and empowered—to live divine lives according to the New Law of Christ.

We know we are living that divine life when we experience "the fruit of the Holy Spirit."

St. Paul describes the "fruit of the Spirit" by listing nine benchmarks that set the standard for normal Christian living. The traits that identify us as authentic Christians in daily life are, *"love, joy, peace, patience, kindness, generosity, faithfulness, gentleness, and self-control"* (Galatians 5:22–23). These are the benchmarks we should constantly keep in mind.

To achieve them, however, we need special divine help. God empowers us to bear the "fruit of the Spirit" by giving us the gifts of the Holy Spirit that Isaiah prophesied Jesus would have:

> A shoot shall come out from the stump of Jesse, and from his roots a bud shall blossom. The spirit of the LORD shall rest on him, the spirit of *Wisdom* and *Understanding*, the spirit of *Counsel* and *Strength*, the spirit of *Knowledge* and *Fear of the LORD*. His delight shall be in the Fear of the LORD. ▪ ISAIAH 11:1FF.

> (*The Septuagint and the Vulgate read "**Piety**" for "Fear of the Lord" in its first occurrence, from which we have the traditional seven gifts.*)

Obviously, if we are serious about living by the Spirit, we need to give serious attention to these gifts. What are they, what do they help us do, and how can we make the best use of them? This book shows us how to grow in holiness by using the gifts of the Holy Spirit so that the fruit of the Holy Spirit will be evident in our lives.

The
GIFTS
OF THE
SPIRIT

TO LIVE BY THE SPIRIT WE NEED THE GIFTS OF THE SPIRIT

Peter said to them, "Repent, and be baptized every one of you in the name of Jesus Christ so that your sins may be forgiven; and you will receive the gift of the Holy Spirit."
ACTS 2:38

We hardly speak of the "gift of the Holy Spirit" today. But in the early Church it was recognized as a major element of the Christian life—so much so, that if someone did not receive the gift of the Spirit at baptism, something had to be done about it.

When the Greek Christians fled to Samaria to escape persecution, they preached the Good News, although they were laypersons. And they baptized converts. When the apostles at Jerusalem heard this, they sent Peter and John to them, who laid their hands on the newly baptized, "and they received the Holy Spirit... for as yet the Spirit had not come upon any of them; they had only been baptized in the name of the Lord Jesus." And when Paul found believers at Ephesus, he asked them, "Did you receive the Holy Spirit when you became believers?" When they replied, "No, we have not even heard that there is a Holy Spirit," Paul "laid his hands on them, the Holy Spirit came upon them, and they spoke in tongues and prophesied" (Acts 8:14–16; 19:2–6).

This was in fulfillment of Jesus's promise to the Apostles (Acts 1:8): "You will receive power when the Holy Spirit has come upon you; and you will be my witnesses in Jerusalem, in all Judea and Samaria, and to the ends of the earth."

Credible witness to the Good News can only be borne by those who show the fruit of the Spirit in their lives. But for this we need to be empowered by the gifts of the Spirit. The letter to the Hebrews (2:4) says God backed up the testimony of Jesus "by signs and wonders and various miracles, and by gifts of the Holy Spirit, distributed according to his will."

It should give us pause that Paul said, "Those who are unspiritual do not receive the gifts of God's Spirit, for they are foolishness to them, and they are unable to understand them because they are spiritually discerned." But formed Christians "have received not the spirit of the world, but the Spirit that is from God, so that we may understand the gifts bestowed on us by God" (1 Corinthians 2:12). And, in fact, Understanding is the second of the seven gifts of the Holy Spirit.

So it is important for us not only to know what the gifts of the Spirit are, but to be able to define them and use them. Only by using the gifts of the Holy Spirit will we be able to live by the Spirit in such a way that the fruit of the Spirit appears in our life.

The Way of
WISDOM

A shoot shall come out from the stump of Jesse, and from his roots a bud shall blossom. The spirit of the LORD shall rest on him, the spirit of Wisdom and Understanding, the spirit of Counsel and Strength, the spirit of Knowledge and Fear of the LORD. His delight shall be in the Fear of the LORD. ISAIAH 11:1FF.

(As stated earlier, the Septuagint and the Vulgate read "Piety"—that is, Family Spirit—for "Fear of the Lord" in its first occurrence, which gives us the traditional seven gifts.)

Four gifts of the Spirit enlighten the intellect: *Wisdom, Understanding, Knowledge,* and *Counsel.* Three strengthen the will: *Family Spirit, Strength,* and *Awe of the Lord.* Wisdom is defined as the habit of seeing everything in the light of our last end.

The striking thing that should shine out in any Christian's life is a *joie de vivre,* an enthusiasm for living that comes from awareness that we have something to live for. Not "pie-in-the-sky when you die," but literally heaven on earth: a joy, a fulfillment that is ours right now, that is increasing, and will be ours completely when our earthly pilgrimage is over.

Our "last end" is something we are tasting now, that gives purpose, meaning, and motivation to everything we do.

For Christians, "heaven" is not a place. It is that "life to the full" that Jesus said he came to give (John 10:10). It is something we believe in and are experiencing in increasing measure right now.

The Christian "heaven" is not human life to the full, such as we might imagine in some modern version of Valhalla or the Happy Hunting Ground. The fullness of life we live for is the Life of God: the ecstatic mutual Oneness of the Three Persons interacting with each other in total awareness of all that is True and Good and Beautiful.

We who have been made divine by "the grace of the Lord Jesus Christ" (2 Corinthians 13:13, words we use to begin Mass) share in that Life now. We are caught up now in the Life of the Trinity, sharing in their communal act of knowing, sharing in their communal act of loving, sharing in the unity they enjoy as totally One in Being, Goodness, and Truth.

We are in heaven now.

True, we don't share in that Life with full consciousness yet.

> For now we see in a mirror, dimly, but then we will see face
> to face. Now we know only in part; then we will know fully,
> even as we have been fully known. ▪ 1 CORINTHIANS 13:12

> Beloved, we are God's children now; what we will be has
> not yet been revealed. What we do know is this: when he is
> revealed, we will be like him, for we will see him as he is.
> ▪ 1 JOHN 3:2

We all received "life to the full" in baptism, when, in the words of St. Augustine, as Christ's body on earth, we "became Christ."

> We have become not only Christians, but Christ himself.
> Do you understand and grasp, brethren, God's grace toward
> us? Marvel and rejoice: we have *become Christ.*
> ▪ SEE CATECHISM OF THE CATHOLIC CHURCH, 795

The Fathers of the Church were so conscious of the divine life we receive at baptism that they took for granted language that shocks us today. St. Athanasius said the Word was "made human so that we might be made God" (*De Incarnatione*, 54.3). Saint Basil the Great (329-379 A.D.) wrote: "Through the Spirit we acquire a likeness to God; indeed, we attain what is beyond our most sublime aspirations—we become God" (Office of Readings, Tuesday of the 7th week of Eastertide).

We are divine. We just have to surrender completely to living fully the Life that is already ours.

Our experience of Jesus is the mystical experience of realizing with Saint Paul that "it is *no longer I who live, but it is Christ who lives in me*" (Galatians 2:20). Jesus is not just a historical figure outside of us to look at and imitate, but the mystery of "*Christ in us, our hope of glory*" (see Colossians 1:27). We are called, not just to "follow" Jesus but to let Christ "be *formed in us*" (Galatians 4:19)—that is, to let his life, his truth, his love grow in us and permeate every part and particularity of our unique human nature and characteristics—until we all "become one in faith and in the knowledge of God's Son, and *form that perfect man* who is *Christ come to full stature*" (Ephesians 4:12–13). This is our "end," what we exist for. It is what the gift of Wisdom helps us to live for consciously.

By definition Christians are seekers—a "pilgrim Church"— and what we are seeking is ever-deepening, ever-expanding experience of the mystery of God—and of ourselves as sharing in the life of God (Romans 6:4; 2 Corinthians 5:17, 6:18). That is our purpose on earth.

> All of us, with unveiled faces, seeing the glory of the Lord
> as though reflected in a mirror, are being transformed into
> the same image from one degree of glory to another; for
> this comes from the Lord, the Spirit. ▪ 2 CORINTHIANS 3:18

This is the mystery of Christian life, a mystery that should be visible in the evident zest for life that Christians have, fired by awareness of purpose and promise. We exist to be drawn into understanding of God's innermost thoughts, to be totally one with God in mind and will and heart.

Awareness of this is the gift of *Wisdom—the gift of seeing everything we do in the light of all we are and are called to be.*

We use the gift of Wisdom by cultivating the habit of seeing everything in the light of our "last end," the goal of our existence, which, as we have seen, we possess already by grace, although we do not yet experience it completely.

Paul shows us Wisdom in action:

> I regard everything as loss because of the surpassing value of knowing Christ Jesus my Lord. For his sake I have suffered the loss of all things, and I regard them as rubbish, in order that I may gain Christ and be found in him. Not that I...have already reached the goal; but I press on to make it my own, because Christ Jesus has made me his own....This one thing I do...I press on toward the goal for the prize of the heavenly call of God in Christ Jesus.
> ▪ PHILIPPIANS 3:8FF.

"I press on toward the goal." That is Wisdom. Conscious intentionality. Purpose. Something to live and hope for, confident we will attain it, because we already possess it.

> A highway will be there, called the holy way;
> No one unclean may pass over it, nor fools go astray on it...
> It is for [the wise] those with a journey to make...
> ▪ ISAIAH 35:8

The key to Wisdom is awareness. Awareness that we already possess what we are living for and are simply growing into it. Awareness that we are living the Life of God. Awareness all day long that God the Son, Jesus, is living in us, acting *with us, in us,* and *through us.* We are already one with God. If we keep ourselves conscious of this, every thought, word, and deed will unite us more intimately with him. And with one another.

Jesus prayed "that they may all be one. As you, Father, are in me and I am in you, may they also be in us … so that they may be one, as we are one" (John 17:21).

That is heaven: the whole human race gathered together around one table at the "wedding banquet of the Lamb" (Revelation 19:9), in total unity of mind and will and heart with God and each other, seeing all that is True and Good and Beautiful in God and in every other human being.

At the end, St. Augustine said, there will be "one Christ, loving himself" (Homily 10, on 1 John 5:1–3). The way of Wisdom is to keep ourselves conscious that we are one with Christ now, and to let him live and love *with us, in us,* and *through us* in every word we speak, every choice we make, every action we perform, longing for the day when all will be perfectly one in him.

This awareness is the first thing that should shine out in any Christian's life: the Wisdom of those who know they have something to live for, and by the power of the Holy Spirit within them are consciously living for it.

Pope Francis said in his homily on Ash Wednesday, March 6, 2019:

> In life's journey, as in every journey, what really matters is
> not to lose sight of the goal. If what interests us as we travel,
> however, is looking at the scenery or stopping to eat, we
> will not get far. We should ask ourselves: On the journey
> of life, do I seek the way forward? Or am I satisfied with

living in the moment and thinking only of feeling good, solving some problems and having fun? What is the path? Is it the search for health, which many today say comes first but which eventually passes? Could it be possessions and well-being? But we are not in the world for this. *Return to me*, says the Lord. To *me*. The Lord is the goal of our journey in this world. The direction must lead to him.

Wisdom also means *appreciation*, desire for what is spiritual.

Wisdom helps us focus on our goal by giving us desire for it. In Latin, Wisdom is *"sapientia"*—from *sapor*, savor. Wisdom is also defined as the gift of "taste" or appreciation for spiritual things.

One who desires the goal will desire the means. So Wisdom, by keeping us conscious of the promise of our destiny, also makes us appreciate all the spiritual helps that lead to its fulfillment.

TO USE THE GIFT OF WISDOM
Form the habit of saying the WIT prayer when you wake up in the morning and all day long, before everything you do: *"Lord, do this **with** me, do this **in** me, do this **through** me."* Add, if you like, *"Let me think with your thoughts and speak with your words and act as your body on earth."*

The Way of
UNDERSTANDING

Now we have received... the Spirit that is from God, so that we may understand the gifts bestowed on us by God. And we speak of these things in words... taught by the Spirit, interpreting spiritual things to those who are spiritual....We have the mind of Christ.

1 CORINTHIANS 2:9FF.

Jesus said to his disciples, "You are the light of the world.... Let your light shine before others, so they may see your good works and give glory to your Father in heaven" (Matthew 5:14, 16).

This means it is just as important for Christians to understand the teachings of Jesus as it is for a doctor to understand medicine. As important as it is for an engineer to understand the structural strengths and weaknesses of a building. Or for an airplane pilot to understand the machine she is flying.

The reason is: lives depend on it.

Christians know that the quality of our spiritual lives depends a great deal on how well we understand and visibly live out the Good News of Jesus. We owe it to others to relay the Good News faithfully. That is a serious responsibility. The bishops at the Second Vatican Council (1962–1965) affirmed it:

> To the extent that believers neglect their own training in the faith, or teach erroneous doctrine, or are deficient in their religious, moral or social life, they must be said to

conceal rather than reveal the authentic face of God and religion. ▪ *THE CHURCH IN THE MODERN WORLD, 19*

Noblesse oblige. It is important—very important—for us to understand the truth entrusted to us so that we can express it faithfully. The fact is, we are the privileged intimates of God!

Paul said, "Think of us in this way, as servants of Christ and stewards of God's mysteries." Peter added: "Like good stewards of the manifold grace of God, serve one another with whatever gift each of you has received" (1 Corinthians 4:1; 1 Peter 4:10).

Jesus said, "From everyone to whom much has been given, much will be required; and from the one to whom much has been entrusted, even more will be demanded" (Luke 12:48). What does he expect of us, to whom he has revealed his whole heart?

He said at the Last Supper: "I do not call you servants any longer….But I have called you friends, because I have made known to you everything that I have heard from my Father" (John 15:15).

THE MYSTERY OF FAITH

Let's not overlook the mystery in this. How can Jesus "make known" to us what he has heard from the Father? Jesus himself said: "No one knows the Son except the Father, and no one knows the Father except the Son" (Matthew 11:27).

By "no one knows" Jesus meant "it is impossible for anyone to know." To know the mystery of God as God really is, you have to be God. To know God the Father as Father you have to *be* God the Son.

Then Jesus added, in apparent self-contradiction, "and anyone to whom the Son chooses to reveal him."

To "reveal him" doesn't mean "tell us about him." Jesus is saying he can give us the same knowledge of the Father that he has—in the only way possible: which is by letting us share in his own personal, divine act, as God the Son, of knowing the Father.

By "grace" we share in God's own act of Being: his Life, "eternal life." But God's Life is to know the True and love the Good. Our sharing in God's act of knowing is the divine gift—the light—of Faith.

The problem is, God knows in a way that is both like and unlike ours. God sees everything in one act, in a single, infinite "Word" of knowledge. We see things in many words—thoughts—one at a time. And we have to put words together into sentences in order to understand.

The Spanish mystic Mary of Agreda, explained this:

> God comprehends in himself all things by one indivisible, most simple and instantaneous act. He does not go from the understanding of one thing to the understanding of another like we do, distinguishing and perceiving first one thing by an act of the understanding, and after that proceeding to the knowledge of others by their connection with those already known. God knows them conjointly all at once, without before and after, since all are together and at once contained in the divine and uncreated knowledge…just as they are comprehended and enclosed in his infinite Being, as in their first beginning.
>
> ▪ THE MYSTICAL CITY OF GOD

To help us translate into conscious, human knowledge the divine knowledge that is in us by the light of Faith, so that we can deal with it, God gives us the gift of the Holy Spirit we call Understanding.

THE GIFT OF UNDERSTANDING

Understanding is just what it says: the gift to understand with our human minds those mysteries that "surpass all understanding" (see Philippians 3:7; Luke 8:10).

> What no eye has seen…nor the human heart conceived…
> these things God has revealed to us through the Spirit….
> No one comprehends what is truly God's except the Spirit
> of God. Now we have received…the Spirit that is from God,
> so that we may understand the gifts bestowed on us by God.
> And we speak of these things in words…taught by the Spirit,
> interpreting spiritual things to those who are spiritual….We
> have the mind of Christ. ▪ 1 CORINTHIANS 2:9FF.

"We have the mind of Christ." That is how we know the Father as only the Son can know him. But we have to use our human minds, our reasons, to reflect on what we know by the mind of Christ— to reflect on everything Jesus has taught us—until we can express it in a way that is understandable to our minds. Then it becomes for us conscious, usable, human knowledge.

That is what meditative prayer is: a process that converts divine knowledge into human understanding.

The gift of Understanding helps us do this. But only if we use it. Too many people don't bother, because they don't understand how important it is.

WE NEED TO KEEP LEARNING

It is not enough—in fact, it is positively harmful—to try to live the Christian life with a superficial understanding of Christian doctrine. A superficial understanding usually means an unreflective and unchallenged acceptance of "cultural Christianity." We "follow the crowd," taking for granted that because it is the Christian crowd, it must be going in the right direction.

And it is, for the most part. The Holy Spirit is keeping us within the channel markers of the essential Christian doctrines. But within those boundaries, Christian teaching and practice is constantly veering off to the left or right, constantly interpreting Christian doctrines in ways that "miss the mark"—in, let's face it, "sinful" ways (the New Testament word for sin is *hamartia*, to "miss")—that are all the more harmful because they are unrecognized.

As we said above, the bishops acknowledged this and warned us against it in the Second Vatican Council. The bishops said a carelessly taught Christianity contributes to the rise of atheism. We see today how a false understanding of Christian doctrine, embodied in distorted rules and practices, has contributed to the proliferation of ex-Christians and "nones"—those who profess no religion at all. According to a 2012 report by the Pew Research Center, "One fifth of the U.S. public—and a third of adults under 30—are religiously unaffiliated," the highest percentage Pew had ever polled. The Vatican II bishops explained it ahead of time: this "stems from a variety of causes, including a critical reaction against religious beliefs, and in some places against the Christian religion in particular. Hence believers can have more than a little to do with the birth of atheism"—and with the death of religion in so many people and places—"to the extent that believers neglect their own training in the faith, or teach erroneous doctrine."

Pope Francis is one of the strongest voices calling us not to accept the *status quo* of cultural Christianity, and never to be satisfied with what we think we understand:

> In the quest to seek and find God in all things there is still an area of uncertainty. There must be. If a person says with total certainty that he has met God, and is not touched by a margin of uncertainty, then this is not good. For me, this is an important key. If one has the answers to all the questions—that is the proof that God is not with him. It means

that he is a false prophet using religion for himself. The great leaders of the people of God, like Moses, have always left room for doubt. We must leave room for the Lord, not [exclude him by] our certainties; we must be humble. Uncertainty is in every true discernment that is open to finding confirmation in spiritual consolation.

A Christian who is a restorationist, a legalist, who wants everything clear and safe, will find nothing. Tradition and memory of the past must help us to have the courage to open up new areas to God. Those who today always look for disciplinarian solutions, those who long for an exaggerated doctrinal "security," those who stubbornly try to recover a past that no longer exists—they have a static and inward-directed view of things. In this way, faith becomes an ideology among other ideologies.

▪ *AMERICA MAGAZINE INTERVIEW, SEPT. 30, 2013*

Because it is normal that a "pilgrim Church" should always be adjusting and correcting its course, the Vatican II bishops "urge all concerned, if any abuses, excesses or defects have crept in here or there, to do what is in their power to remove or correct them, and to restore all things to a fuller praise of Christ and of God" (*Constitution on the Church*, 51).

Pope Francis is saying that, to do this today, we need an attitude open to change.

The first reform must be our attitude. The ministers of the Gospel must be people who can warm the hearts of the people, who walk through the dark night with them, who know how to dialogue and to descend themselves into their people's night, into the darkness, but without getting lost....They must also be able to accompany the flock that has a flair for finding new paths.

> Instead of being just a Church that welcomes and
> receives by keeping the doors open, let us try also to be a
> Church that finds new roads, that is able to step outside
> itself and go to those who do not attend Mass, to those who
> have quit or are indifferent. The ones who quit sometimes
> do it for reasons that, if properly understood and assessed,
> can lead to a return. But that takes audacity and courage.
>
> ▪ AMERICA MAGAZINE INTERVIEW SEPTEMBER 30, 2013

To do what we need to do today we have to use the gift of Understanding. We must assume that we do not fully understand—and in some cases positively misunderstand—authentic teaching. If we are simply living the cultural Christianity we grew up with, we are the half blind following the half blind along a way that distorts the truth and diminishes the life that Jesus—the authentic Way, Truth, and Life (John 14:6)—holds out to all who follow him. Faith without understanding is the light of the blind.

FAITHFUL STEWARDSHIP

God obviously wants us to use God's gifts. Scripture makes that clear: "To each is given the manifestation of the Spirit for the common good." So, "like good stewards of the manifold grace of God, serve one another with whatever gift each of you has received" (1 Corinthians 12:7; 1 Peter 4:10).

We all have a special gift of the Holy Spirit to help us understand what we have learned. We need to use it.

"Do not neglect the gift that is in you....Rekindle the gift of God" (1 Timothy 4:14; 2 Timothy 1:6). We must not let the gifts of the Holy Spirit lie idle in us, forgotten and ineffective. We must use them, not only for ourselves but for others. It is our Christian duty—a ministry of love—to be able to explain everything we believe. The first pope said what the current pope is saying! "Always be ready to make your defense to anyone who demands from you an accounting for the hope that is in you" (1 Peter 3:15).

It is love to "strive for the spiritual gifts," and to "strive to excel in them for building up the Church" (1 Corinthians 14:1,12).

Jesus said to us all: "You are the light of the world...let your light shine before others" (Matthew 5:14, 16). To do this, we need the gift of Understanding.

And we need to use it. We do that when we become *disciples,* which does not mean "followers" of Jesus but *students.* The only authentic disciples of Jesus Christ are those who have committed themselves in concrete ways to keep studying the mind and heart of God—for example, by reading and reflecting on the words of God in Scripture. These are the ones who take the gift of Understanding seriously.

TO USE THE GIFT OF UNDERSTANDING

Practice asking, "What does this mean?" every time you hear or think about any Church doctrine or practice. Most are mysteries, so don't settle for pat phrases.

We use all sorts of words correctly in sentences without really understanding what they mean. Intellectual clarity depends mostly on understanding better the meaning of individual words. For example, take what you hear at Mass:

- "The grace of our Lord Jesus Christ." What is "grace"?
- "Communion in the Holy Spirit." What is that?
- Why do we call the priest at the altar the "presider"? What does the congregation do?
- What, precisely, is the main thing happening at Mass? How are we involved in that action? Do you know the meaning of the words you use to explain it?

Don't just listen attentively to the words at Mass; listen reflectively. Listen for the mystery in them, for their full meaning. Ask how they change your understanding of yourself, of what Christianity really is. Ask what difference they should make in your life.

Try reading Scripture. The meaning is usually pretty obvious. But some texts are "truths that invite endless exploration" (the definition of mystery). The more you look at them with the eyes of your mind open, the more you see. You experience the gift of Understanding.

Read books on spirituality—especially the ones based on "theology" defined as "Faith seeking understanding." (Begin with the books listed on www.immersedinChrist.org!)

And keep up with the ongoing dialogue in the Church. Use the Internet. Get the Pope App (free). Go to *La Croix International* (subscribe@international.la-croix.com), to NCRonline.org, to americamagazine.org, or to cathnews.co.nz to see what is being said and discussed today by those attentive to the Spirit. (Judge for yourself if they are!)

Ask the Holy Spirit for guidance. Ask for the gift of Understanding.

You may not have all the answers, but if you keep asking the questions, you will never be bored again!

The Way of
KNOWLEDGE

*Teach me to do your will....Let your good spirit lead me
on a level path.* PSALM 143:10

The difference between the gifts of Understanding
and Knowledge is the difference between theory
and practice. Knowledge is practical "know-how"
in the spiritual life. It shows us how to use to best
advantage everything God has given us.

The truth of Christian theory—on the level of revealed doctrine at least—is guaranteed by God. But the way Christians live
out what they believe, and often the way they are taught—or
simply not taught—to put into practice the mysteries of faith, frequently falls far short of the ideal.

TO "SIN" MEANS TO "FALL SHORT"

In the New Testament, the word used for "sin" is *hamartia*: to
"miss the mark" or "fall short." If sometimes we feel we are being
shortchanged in what we get out of our religion—the Mass, the
sacraments, preaching, prayer—or that Christian teachings fall
short in giving us the satisfaction, peace, or motivation we desire,
we should at least ask whether we ourselves are falling short in
the use we make of them. The gift of Knowledge teaches us how
to get the most out of everything we are offered, invited to do, or
just have to put up with.

We need to use the gift.

So ask yourself now how well you are putting into practice what you believe: How much do you get out of Mass? How much do you put into it? Do you know how to participate "fully, consciously, and actively"? The Vatican II bishops wrote:

> In order that the liturgy may be able to produce its full effects, it is necessary that the faithful come to it with proper dispositions, that their minds should be attuned to their voices, and that they should cooperate with divine grace lest they receive it in vain. Pastors of souls must therefore realize that, when the liturgy is celebrated, something more is required than the mere observation of the laws governing valid and licit celebration; *it is their duty also to ensure that the faithful take part fully aware of what they are doing, actively engaged in the rite, and enriched by its effects...*
>
> Mother Church earnestly desires that all the faithful should be led to that *fully conscious, and active participation* in liturgical celebrations which is demanded by the very nature of the liturgy. Such participation by the Christian people as "a chosen race, a royal priesthood, a holy nation, a redeemed people" (1 Peter 2:4–9), is their *right and duty* by reason of their Baptism.
>
> In the restoration and promotion of the sacred liturgy, this full and active participation by all the people is the aim to be considered before all else; for it is the primary and indispensable source from which the faithful are to derive the true Christian spirit; and therefore pastors of souls must zealously strive to achieve it, by means of the necessary instruction, in all their pastoral work.
>
> ▪ *CONSTITUTION ON THE SACRED LITURGY* 11, 14

Are you using the sacrament of reconciliation in a way that helps you grow? What do you focus on in your examination of conscience: the Ten Commandments or the "fruits of the Spirit" that show you are living by the New Law of Christ?

Is your "penance" something that really helps you change?

How do you live out baptism in daily life? What keeps you conscious you have "become Christ"? How do you live out the gift of divine life?

If asked, could you define instantly the "job description" of a Christian? It is summarized in three words in the *Rite of Baptism*. Do you know what are they are? (Hint: What does the minister say when anointing with chrism?) Could you describe what it means in practice, in ordinary daily life, to do your job as prophet, priest, and steward of the kingship of Christ?

What difference does the sacrament of confirmation make in your life? What practical effects is it having now?

What help are you getting from the sacrament of matrimony? Does every day of your marriage bring you closer to your children and spouse?

Do you know how to read Scripture? How to reflect on and pray over what you have read?

Do you look forward to going to work every day because you know you are enriching others' lives—now and forever?

Are all of your friendships mutually inspiring?

Do you know how to grow through anxiety and suffering into deeper faith, hope, and love?

Are you looking forward to death as the greatest free moment of life? How are you preparing to speak your full, final, and irrevocable "Yes!" to God? The "Yes!" that will be your cry of ecstasy forever?

Some people hire a trainer for physical fitness. Do you have a spiritual director?

The examples above are just samples of the things the gift of Knowledge teaches us to do. If we learn how to use this gift—and the Holy Spirit helps us "know how"—we will learn how to use everything in life in a way that brings us to greater fulfillment. Jesus said, "I came that they might have life, and have it to the full" (John 10:10). The gift of Knowledge shows us how.

So how do we use the gift that shows us how to use the gifts?

TO USE THE GIFT OF KNOWLEDGE

First, be aware you have it. You can't google for an answer if you don't know you are on the internet. So form the habit of "googling" the Spirit constantly to ask how to do what you are about to do.

Second, look for practical results. If you "don't get anything" out of Mass, prayer, the sacraments, and everything else you do in life, ask the Spirit to show you why. Life is too short to waste effort. "Whether you eat or drink, or whatever you do, do everything for the glory of God" (1 Corinthians 10:31). Keep checking to see if you actually are.

All Three Persons of the Holy Trinity guarantee results: Jesus said, "I chose you to bear fruit.... The Father will give you whatever you ask him in my name... and the Holy Spirit will teach you" (see John 14:26; 15:16). So call on the gift of Knowledge with confidence that God will show you how to live.

Then use your brains and think.

Of course, sometimes what God inspires us to do is to seek advice from a more experienced Christian or spiritual director. And there are books that help. (This is one of them.)

A FEW "TRICKS OF THE TRADE"

- To keep in touch with God all day long, use "rinky-dink prayer," asking God for things too unimportant to bother the Almighty with: prayers like "Where did I leave my glasses?" "Please help me find a parking spot." When God helps you, say "thank you."

- To grow into awareness of the mystery of your identification with Christ, say the WIT prayer all day long: "Lord, do this *with* me, do this *in* me, do this *through* me."
- To experience your commitment to discipleship, put a Bible on your pillow. Promise God never to go to sleep without reading *one line.*
- At Mass, *pay attention to the words.* They are exciting! You will never be bored again.
- To prepare for confession, don't just look for sins. Ask how you are using the gifts of the Holy Spirit. Ask whether the fruit of the Spirit (Galatians 5:22) is visible in your life. Where it isn't, ask why. That will show you where you are failing.
- To live out your confirmation and your baptismal anointing to bear witness as *prophet*, never ask again whether something is right or wrong. Ask instead, "How does this bear witness to the values of Christ?"
- To live out your baptismal anointing to ministry as *priest*, begin by forming the habit of praising everybody for everything good you see in them. Begin with your spouse and family. See what this does for your marriage.
- To be faithful to your baptismal anointing to work for change as a *king*, or *steward* of the kingship of Christ, form the habit of just *noticing* anything around you that doesn't reflect the reign of God. Try to change what you reasonably can.
- Adopt the routine of praying very briefly five times a day: 1. When you wake; 2. When you get out of bed; 3. At noon; 4. Before, during, or after supper; 5. Before you go to sleep. For concrete suggestions, go to the website www. immersedinChrist.org.

The Way of
COUNSEL

"The Advocate, the Holy Spirit, whom the Father will send in my name, will teach you everything, and remind you of all that I have said to you." JOHN 14:26

The gift of Counsel is assistance in making decisions for which my normal level of reason and common sense are not enough. For example, between two good choices, which is the better? Or between two bad choices, which is the lesser of two evils? What does God want me to do?

John's gospel calls the Holy Spirit the "Paraclete" (14:16, 26; 15:26; 16:7), which means "called to one's side." We often translate it as Advocate, which has the suggestion of "lawyer," although it is much more than that.

In court, lawyers are referred to as "counsel." Most people have a working knowledge of the law that is sufficient for daily life. But in difficult situations they are advised to "take counsel." When Christians need help to make a decision, they "call to their side" the Holy Spirit, the "Counselor."

Using the Holy Spirit in decision making is called "discernment." It doesn't replace common sense or dispense us from ascertaining the facts and clarifying our understanding of Church teaching. We use discernment especially when reason and education are not enough.

For Christians, this is an ongoing experience. We are not on earth to live a good human life. We have been reborn as the body of Christ to live a divine life and let Jesus continue his divine life and mission in us. Our life is to let Jesus act *with us, in us,* and *through us.* That means to be guided by his Spirit. "For all who are led by the Spirit of God are children of God" (Romans 8:14). And for that we need discernment—and the gift of Counsel.

Jesus was led by the Spirit:

> Jesus, full of the Holy Spirit...was led by the Spirit in the wilderness....Then Jesus, filled with the power of the Spirit, returned to Galilee. ▪ LUKE 4:1, 14

He promised that his apostles would also be led by the Spirit:

> "For it is not you who speak, but the Spirit...speaking through you....When the Spirit of truth comes, he will guide you into all the truth." ▪ MATTHEW 10:20; JOHN 16:13

The guidance of the Holy Spirit was taken for granted in the early Church. For example:

> Then the Spirit said to Philip, "Go over to this chariot and join it"....When they came up out of the water, the Spirit of the Lord snatched Philip away....They attempted to go into Bithynia, but the Spirit of Jesus did not allow them....If we live by the Spirit, let us also be guided by the Spirit....
> ▪ ACTS 8:29, 39; 16:7; GALATIANS 5:25

The Christian life is a life of experienced union with God bolstered by conscious recognition of inspirations from the Holy Spirit. Knowing that we should expect inspirations helps us recognize them when they come.

The point is, the gift of Counsel is standard equipment for a

Christian. We should make constant use of it in daily life: asking for light from the Holy Spirit when we make decisions, keeping alert to feelings or inclinations that might be inspirations from God, and staying aware at all times that Christ wants to act *with us, in us,* and *through us* in everything we do.

Christians never ask just whether something is right or wrong, but whether it is what the Spirit is moving us to do at this moment. A practical way to discern this is to ask before everything we say, do, buy, or use: "How does this bear witness to the values of Christ?"

Prudence is a human virtue by which we make good human choices. Counsel is a gift of the Spirit by which we make divine choices. Christians live by the gifts of the Spirit. Not to do so is to live a sub-Christian life.

But we need to make divine living a habit.

TO USE THE GIFT OF COUNSEL

Remember, we are always called to do the impossible: to live and act on the level of God. So we always need the help and Counsel of the Holy Spirit.

> "Be perfect, therefore, as your heavenly Father is perfect."
> ▪ MATTHEW 5:48

> Do not be conformed to this world, but be transformed by the renewing of your minds, so that you may discern what is the will of God—what is good and acceptable and perfect. ▪ ROMANS 12:2

> Jesus looked at them and said, "For mortals it is impossible, but for God all things are possible." ▪ MATTHEW 19:26

First, form the habit of always asking the Father, Son, or Spirit for help in every decision you make.

Second, include the Prayer to the Holy Spirit in your morning prayer. (It is worth the time to memorize this expanded version):

> Come Holy Spirit, fill the hearts of your faithful, and enkindle in us the fire of your divine love. Send forth your Spirit, Lord, and *our hearts will be regenerated. And you will renew the face of the earth.*
>
> Lord, by the light of the Holy Spirit you instruct the hearts of your faithful. Grant us, by the gifts of *Wisdom, Understanding, Knowledge, Counsel, Family Spirit, Strength,* and *Awe of the Lord,* that we will "not be conformed to this world," but "transformed by the renewal of our minds," so that we might discern and do what is "good, and pleasing to God, and perfect," and so be the "aroma of Christ" in the world through the fruits of the Holy Spirit:
>
> *Love, Joy, Peace,*
> *Patient Endurance, Kindness, Generosity,*
> *Faithfulness, Gentleness,* and the *Self-Control*
> of total surrender to your Spirit.

Third, learn to use the "Awareness Exercise." This is a way to become aware of how God is interacting with us in countless ways all day long, and especially when we pray. God inspires, invites, guides, and cautions us. But God doesn't shout or shove; God nudges and whispers. God respects our freedom too much to identify himself openly as God speaking until he knows we want to hear what he says. All we have to do to ignore God is just not listen very hard. The Awareness Exercise is a way to listen, to identify God's action in our hearts and our response to it.

THE AWARENESS EXERCISE

To begin, pause for a moment, clear your mind, recall the presence of God, and ask God to help you.

Then, *get in touch with your feelings*. Feelings are never good or bad, because they are not free acts. But they can be useful to tell us which way the wind is blowing in our hearts, and the wind may be the Holy Spirit. So look for any change you have experienced in your mood or feelings during the day or during your prayer. "How did I feel when I began this day (or meditation)? How do I feel now? Did my mood change at any moment? Was it because of some thought I had? Did I make a choice I feel good about? Or one I do not feel at peace with? Has any thought been bugging me? Is there something I need to reconsider, look at more deeply?"

Next, *make a judgment* about the source of those feelings. Is there some obvious natural explanation? Or could God be assuring you that you are on course by giving you peace? Or is he perhaps disturbing your peace to warn you that you are getting off course? Have the courage to take a stance toward the decisions and choices of the day, to decide they were right, wrong, or doubtful. You don't have to be absolutely certain, but come to a decision and see if you feel at peace with it.

Then speak to God about *what you are going to do now*. Look to the future. Change any choice God is asking you to change. Take a deliberate stance of faith, encouragement, and love. Ask Jesus to be your Way. Surrender to him.

▪ EXCERPTED FROM "WAYS TO PRAY" AT WWW.IMMERSED-INCHRIST.ORG.

Give about ten minutes a day to this. You can do it during your shower!

The Way of
FAMILY SPIRIT
(OR "PIETY")

"There is no one who has left house or brothers or sisters or mother or father or children or fields, for my sake and for the sake of the Good News, who will not receive a hundredfold now in this age—houses, brothers and sisters, mothers and children." MARK 10:29

Four gifts of the Spirit enlighten the intellect: *Wisdom, Understanding, Knowledge,* and *Counsel.* Three strengthen the will: *Family Spirit, Strength,* and *Awe of the Lord.* The gift of *Family Spirit* is a Christian's ongoing motivation to do what is "right and just" in the ordinary circumstances of daily life. *Strength* helps us in special situations to do what is difficult or dangerous. *Awe of the Lord* helps us to not do what is wrong when our desires incline us to it.

On the human level, the basic inclination that drives people of good will to act properly toward each other from day to day might be an underlying commitment to justice—a human predisposition to "fair play" and respect for everyone's rights. But for Christians it is a faith-grounded, divine commitment to Family Love and Loyalty. Our basic desire is to show the love of brother or sister, father or mother, to everyone in the human race.

The gift of Family Spirit is a divine version of what the Romans called "piety": the gut-bond of loyalty to parents and family—and, by extension, to friends, neighbors, and fellow citizens—that is, to all those we see as "us" as opposed to "them."

31

Piety, as loyalty to one's family, country, and country's gods, was the strength of the Roman Empire. It was modeled in Rome's epic hero, Virgil's *pius Aeneas*.

Jesus extended this Family Spirit to include the whole human race—to embrace all who are, or are called to be, children of God the Father, our brothers and sisters in Christ. This is a loyalty that is not just human but divine, not just cultural but mystical. It is a gift of the Holy Spirit.

This gift inclines our wills to treat everyone with the same love and respect we give to our blood relatives: father and mother, brothers and sisters, cousins, uncles, and aunts. "In Christ" we are all one family. Jesus said:

> "You have heard that it was said, 'You shall love your neighbor and hate your enemy.' But I say to you, 'Love your enemies and pray for those who persecute you,' so that you may be children of your Father in heaven."
> ▪ MATTHEW 5:43–45

> "Truly I tell you, there is no one who has left house or brothers or sisters or mother or father or children or fields, for my sake and for the sake of the Good News, who will not receive a hundredfold now in this age—houses, brothers and sisters, mothers and children…." ▪ MARK 10:29–30

St. Paul and other New Testament writers are explicit about the relationship we have with each other:

> All the brothers and sisters send greetings…and all the members of God's family who are with me….
> ▪ 1 CORINTHIANS 16:20; GALATIANS 1:2

The one who sanctifies and those who are sanctified all
have one Father. For this reason Jesus is not ashamed to call
them brothers and sisters. ▪ HEBREWS 2:11

You have clothed yourselves with the new self....In that
renewal there is no longer Greek and Jew, circumcised and
uncircumcised, barbarian, Scythian, slave and free; but
Christ is all and in all! ▪ COLOSSIANS 3:10, GALATIANS 3:28

Any place where there are Christians should be known as *"phil-adelphia"*—a place of "family love." In all ordinary dealings with
other people, every Christian should stand out for treating every-one as a brother or sister. The gift of Family Spirit should make
this second nature. Christians don't have employers or employ-ees, clients or customers; only family members with whom we do
business. If there are those we don't approve of, even politicians,
we should speak of them—and want others to speak of them—as
we would speak of a brother or sister we don't agree with: with
respect and "steadfast love." This is Loyalty in the Holy Spirit
(Exodus 34:6; John 1:17, *New American Bible,* 1970 edition).

No matter what anyone does, by the gift of Family Spirit we
never forget that the offender is our brother or sister.

"Take heed to yourselves. If your brother sins against you,
rebuke him; and if he repents, forgive him." ▪ LUKE 17:3

If we remembered this, we would never apply the death penalty.

The same is true of people in need. For Christians there are
no "poor people," "foreigners," or "immigrants," just sisters and
brothers who are poor, live in another country, or have sought
refuge here. This is the standard by which we judge ourselves:
the Family Spirit of Loyalty to our brothers and sisters in Christ,
Loyalty to fellow children of our Father.

How does God's love abide in anyone who has the world's goods and sees a brother or sister in need and yet refuses help? ▪ 1 JOHN 3:17

TO USE THE GIFT OF FAMILY SPIRIT

As you pray the Our Father, consciously ask whom you are including in the "our."

Whenever you talk to other people—or about them—be conscious they are your brothers and sisters. Also be conscious of it when you serve them or they serve you.

In your business dealings with other people, treat them all as you would your brother or sister.

When you discuss how our laws should deal with other people—immigrants, the poor, or even criminals—imagine you are talking about your own children or blood relatives. Remember that "blood is *not* thicker than water" when we are speaking of the water of baptism.

When anyone succeeds in some good enterprise, be as glad as you would be if it were your blood brother or sister.

Make it your chosen desire to include as many different kinds of people as you can in any community you belong to. Rejoice with St. Paul that:

> The Gentiles [people of all sorts] have become fellow heirs, members of the same body, and sharers in the promise in Christ Jesus through the gospel. ▪ EPHESIANS 3:6

Try, like Jesus, not to be ashamed to treat anyone openly as your brother or sister (Hebrews 2:11).

The Way of
STRENGTH
(COURAGE, FORTITUDE)

"Peace I leave with you; my peace I give to you.
I do not give to you as the world gives. Do not let your hearts
be troubled, and do not let them be afraid."
JOHN 14:27

When fear of consequences or reluctance to undertake something that will cost a lot of time and effort makes us hold back, the gift of Strength gives us help to say "Yes." And to keep saying it. To persevere.

As Christians we are called to bear witness to Christ. If we are authentic, that can be dangerous. The Greek word for "witness" is "martyr," which took on its current meaning because so many of the first Christians were killed for the witness they bore.

To bear witness to the Good News, we need divine Strength.

Paul urges us, "Do not be conformed to this world. Be transformed by the renewing of your minds, so that you may discern what is good, and acceptable, and perfect" (Romans 12:2). If we are not conformed to this world, trying to show the "fruit of the Spirit" by living according to the divine ideals of Christ's New Law (e.g., the Sermon on the Mount, Matthew, chapters 5 to 7) instead of settling for the good human life of the Ten Commandments, we won't "fit in" anymore. And there will be consequences.

"If you belonged to the world, the world would love you as its own. But because...I have chosen you out of the world, the world hates you....If they persecuted me, they will persecute you." ■ JOHN 15:18FF.

But Jesus says, "Do not fear." He promises the gift of the Spirit:

"When they hand you over, do not worry...for what you are to say will be given to you at that time. It is not you who speak, but the Spirit of your Father speaking through you....You will be hated by all because of my name. But the one who endures to the end will be saved."
■ MATTHEW 10:19FF.

Pope Paul VI said, "The first means of evangelization is the witness of an authentically Christian life." An authentic Christian lifestyle is one that raises eyebrows:

Take a Christian or a handful of Christians who...radiate faith in values that go beyond current values, and hope in something not seen, that one would not dare to imagine. Through this wordless witness they stir up irresistible questions in the hearts of those who see how they live: Why are they like this? Why do they live in this way? What or who is it that inspires them?...Such a witness is already a silent proclamation of the Good News.
■ EVANGELIZATION IN THE MODERN WORLD, 21, 41

Many people are threatened by lifestyles that call their own lives into question. When others' reaction to us makes us feel a need for the gift of Strength, we know we are following the gospel.

We also need Strength to "dream the impossible dream"—to take on the Christian task of bringing about cultural change.

Pope John Paul II called for "a detailed pastoral plan" on the level of "the local churches" (dioceses and parishes) that will form lay Christians to "have a deep and incisive influence in bringing Gospel values to bear in society and culture" (*Novo Millennio Ineunte*, January 6, 2001). This is the specific mission of the laity. Parishes should form all their members to fulfill it.

THE APOSTOLATE OF THE LAITY

The bishops said in the Second Vatican Council:

> It is proper to lay Christians' state of life to spend their days in the midst of the world and of secular transactions. They are called there by God to burn with the spirit of Christ and to exercise their apostolate in the world as a kind of leaven.
>
> Laypeople should also know that it is generally the function of their well-formed conscience to see that the divine law is inscribed in the life of the earthly city....Enlightened by Christian wisdom...*let the laity take on their own distinctive role.*
>
> The laity must take on *the renewal of this world* as their own special obligation....Let them act directly and definitively in the temporal sphere...using their own particular skills and acting on their own responsibility. (Vatican II: *Constitution on the Church*, defining the "laity," number 31; *Constitution on the Church in the Modern World*, no. 43; *Decree on the Apostolate of the Laity*, nos. 2, 7. For a modern application of this read Pope Francis' letters *Laudato Si': On Care for Our Common Home* and *Fratelli Tutti: On Fraternity and Social Friendship.*)

To try to reform attitudes, values, or policies in family and social life, business, and politics—and in the Church—we need the gift of Strength: first, because it seems impossible; second, because anyone who works for change will pay a price.

On the other hand, Jesus has assured us, "For God all things are possible" (Matthew 19:26). "I have said this to you, so that in me you may have peace. In the world you face persecution. But take courage; I have overcome the world!" (John 16:33).

There are many reasons why we might decide to do or not do something. But for Christians, fear should never be one of them.

TO USE THE GIFT OF STRENGTH

Ask yourself how often you call on the Holy Spirit for Strength to do what you should. If you don't feel the need for divine help very often, you may not be living a fully Christian life.

In particular, ask where you experience challenge in being a Christian. Not the ordinary human challenge of keeping the Ten Commandments, but the specifically Christian challenge of:

- Living the divine life described in Christ's New Law (for example, in Matthew, chapters 5 to 7);
- Being different by not conforming to the cultural values of your peer group;
- Taking on the divine mission of bringing society under the reign of God by working for changes in family and social life, business, church, and politics.

Begin to notice what needs to be changed around you. Even when you can't do anything about it, just noticing what calls for action is already an experience of taking responsibility.

Face your fears. Again, not the ordinary fears of human life, but your fear of the reactions you might get if you just try to live the gospel completely—and more so if you encourage others to do it with you.

What are the things you don't say or do because you are afraid you won't "fit in"?

Is there any work you feel called to do but have never had the confidence to get involved in?

If you live out what you believe, what might you lose? What will you lose if you don't?

Pray for the gift of Strength, and see if your feelings change.

The Way of
AWE OF THE LORD
(FEAR OF THE LORD)

The fear of the LORD is the beginning of wisdom;
all those who practice it have a good understanding.
The fear of the LORD is hatred of evil.
Pride and arrogance and the way of evil and perverted speech I hate.
PSALM 111:10; PROVERBS 8:13

What would fear be without the emotion of fright?

The answer is "perspective." A truck driver is not frightened by the freeway. But he would not drive on the wrong side of the road at night with his lights off. He knows how big an eighteen-wheeler is and how hard it hits at seventy miles an hour. He is not about to risk a head-on collision. He would simply call it insanity to go against traffic. That is perspective. It is fear without the emotion of fright.

We should not be afraid of God. But we should keep God in perspective: God's Power compared to ours, God's Goodness and Knowledge compared to ours, God's Love compared to ours. We should see it as insanity to go against God.

The gift of appreciating that is called "Awe of the Lord."

By this gift we stand in Awe of God's power—the power to create the earth, the sun, the billions of stars; the power barely glimpsed in earthquakes, hurricanes, volcanoes, tsunamis, and ocean storms.

We stand in awe of God's Truth: God's knowledge and

intelligence. God the Son is the "Word," the *Logos*, the intelligibility behind everything we study in bio*logy*, geo*logy*, cosmo*logy*, anthropo*logy*, ophthalmo*logy*, theo*logy*...

> All things came into being through him, and without
> him not one thing came into being....In him all things in
> heaven and on earth were created, things visible and invisi-
> ble...through him and for him...and in him all things hold
> together. ▪ JOHN 1:3; COLOSSIANS 1:16–17

Even more, we stand in Awe of God's Goodness; and especially of the love God showed by paying the price of sharing divine Life with us:

> "For God so loved the world that he gave his only Son, so
> that everyone who believes in him may not perish but may
> have eternal life....No one has greater love than this, to lay
> down one's life for one's friends." ▪ JOHN 3:16; 15:13

In and throughout and underlying all of this, we stand in Awe of God's Being. We know that of ourselves, we are nothing. Everything we experience as our being came from nothingness. There is nothing in us that explains the fact we exist. The only reason we can say we "are" is that we happen to be. And the only explanation for that is that somewhere, somehow, there is Someone who can say absolutely—as a fact that simply has to be, that requires and admits of no explanation—"*I Am Who Am*" (Exodus 3:14; John 8:58). To be intelligible, the existence of creatures requires the existence of Someone whose very Essence it is to Exist, whose Existence requires no explanation.

That Being, whose Nature it is to Be, is the explanation of why we are. And of why we continue to be. The One who created us said, "Be!"—and is holding the note: "Beeeeee....!" If

God should cough, we would simply cease to exist. And so would everything else—except God. Nothing else has in itself anything that explains its existence. The existence of everything we see requires an explanation. Not so with God.

God is that Being about whose Existence we cannot ask "Why?" If we could see God as God is, we would know that God Is because God Is. It is God's Nature to Be.

As a free gift, out of pure love, God created us—from nothing. That is awesome. But it gets more awesome yet. Not content to give us human existence, human life, as our Creator, God has shared divine Existence with us, God's own divine Life, as our Father.

We who came to be in time now exist for all eternity; God has shared with us God's own eternal life. We live now not just by God's continuing act of keeping us in existence; we live by the Life of God—by God's Eternal life given to us, shared with us.

This is "the grace of the Lord Jesus Christ" (2 Corinthians 13:13). With Saint Paul, every Christian says, "I live now, no longer I; rather, Christ lives in me" (Galatians 2:20).

We live "in Christ," as members of his body, as branches who live by the life of the vine (Romans 12:4; 1 Corinthians 12:12; John 15:4). Paul exhorts us, "As you therefore have received Christ Jesus the Lord, continue to live your lives in him" (Colossians 2:6)—as he is living his Life in us. The mystery of our being, the mystery Paul was sent to preach, he summed up in three words: "Christ in you." And he added, "the hope of glory" (Colossians 1:27).

The "grace of the Lord Jesus Christ" is the favor of sharing in the divine life of God.

That is awesome.

As Christians, we know all this. So how can we possibly go against the infinite power, infinite knowledge and wisdom, infinite love, the infinite Being of God? We would have to be crazy! Everything good is found in God. There is nothing good outside of God. So why do we look for anything else? What do we think we will find by separating ourselves from God?

But we do it. We actually go against the will of the all-powerful God by sinning. We go against the instructions of the all-wise God by preferring our way to God's way. We call into question the goodness of the all-loving God by complaining about things God allows to happen in this world. We ignore the teaching of the *Logos*, the Word, the Truth of God made flesh, by not reading the Scriptures.

We have to be out of our minds!

Oddly enough, in some ways, ever since God has revealed Godself to us more clearly, we are more forgetful of God. The people we call "primitive" did a lot of guessing about God. They were superstitious. But they had a keen sense of perspective. They knew Someone vastly greater than themselves made and owned the land they lived on, the lakes they fished. They paid God homage as best they could. They never just ignored God.

We do. Although it is illogical, the knowledge we have of God that delivers us from superstition also delivers us from healthy Fear of the Lord. We know enough not to be afraid of God but not enough to stand in Awe.

Also, our tiny grasp of technology gives us the impression we understand the universe. The fact we have achieved impressive control over some things makes us claim control over all things. We assume that whatever we can do we have the right to do.

Those who think like that, Scripture calls fools: "Fools say in their hearts, 'There is no God.'" Or they just ignore the fact there is one (Psalm 14:1).

The gift of Awe of the Lord corrects that. While Christianity "makes lonely flesh welcome to creation," the gift of Awe makes us continue to "walk humbly with our God" (Micah 6:8; see Christopher Fry's play, *Thor, With Angels*).

TO USE THE GIFT OF AWE OF THE LORD

Cultivate reverence for God. Never use the name of God without respect. If anyone around you does, bow your head, put your hand on your heart, or make some other sign of reverence. Anyone who resents that is claiming the freedom to insult your God while denying you the freedom to honor God.

Never pass in front of the tabernacle in church without genuflecting or bowing.

Never presume to deny what God says is true, or to act against what God says is good.

It is okay to question what God says, does, or allows, and even to argue with God, but always begin by affirming that you know God is all wise and all loving. We argue with God only for the sake of clarification and to show we take God seriously.

When tempted to choose or use any creature against God's will, remember that the only thing that keeps you from reverting to nothingness is God's ongoing, present choice to keep on giving you existence. Above all, when tempted to use power against another person, recall that you have no power to breathe, think, speak, move, or act in any way except the power God is giving you. Ask Jesus to act *with you, in you,* and *through you* in everything you do. He is the vine. As a branch, apart from him you can do nothing (John 15:5).

As much as you can, avoid anything that gives you prestige or makes you look more important than others. Your greatest dignity is the divine life that makes you a son or daughter of God. In God's family, no child of the Father is higher than another except Jesus. And he, "though he was in the form of God, did not regard equality with God as something to be exploited, but emptied himself, taking the form of a slave, being born in human likeness" (Philippians 2:6–7). Jesus said, "The greatest among you will be your servant. All who exalt themselves will be humbled, and all who humble themselves will be exalted" (Matthew 23:11–12).

Awe of the Lord helps us keep ourselves in perspective.

The

FRUITS

OF THE

SPIRIT

THEY WILL KNOW WE ARE CHRISTIANS BY—THE FRUIT OF THE SPIRIT

But thanks be to God, who... through us spreads in every place the fragrance that comes from knowing him. For we are the aroma of Christ to God among those who are being saved....

2 CORINTHIANS 2:14–17

What does it really mean to be a Christian? If we are living authentic Christian lives, we should be the "aroma of Christ" in the world. That is, wherever we are, whatever we do and say, people should feel in our presence what they felt in the presence of Jesus.

Our friends should feel this. Our family. Our children. Those we work with. To some extent, even the people we pass on the street.

There should be something about us—an aura?—that is not just human goodness but divine.

Our mission, our privilege, and our duty as Christians, is to make the beauty of Christ visible in all of us who are his physical presence on earth. Paul says that through us Jesus "spreads in every place the fragrance that comes from knowing him. For we are the aroma of Christ" (2 Corinthians 2:14–17). If we are not the "aroma of Christ," we are not living authentically Christian lives, no matter how perfectly we keep the Ten Commandments or how frequently we plunk our bodies in the pews.

How do we know whether we are the aroma of Christ? It is simple. We ask whether the "fruit of the Spirit" is evident in our lives.

"Every good tree bears good fruit, but the bad tree bears bad fruit.... Thus you will know them by their fruits."

 • MATTHEW 7:17, 20

The fruit of the Spirit is Love, Joy, Peace, Patient Endurance, Kindness, Generosity, Faithfulness, Gentleness, and Self-Control. • GALATIANS 5:22–23

When we evaluate our lives as Christians, we should not begin by looking for our "sins." Our first question should be, "Is the fruit of the Spirit visible in my life? Do people see me, above all, as *loving*? Do they sense a deep, underlying *joy* in me, even when things are not going well? Do I give the impression of being at *peace* with myself and seeking peace with everyone around me?

"The fruit of the Spirit is Love, Joy, Peace..."

When people try my patience, do I respond with positive acts of kindness—sometimes almost shocking in their generosity? "The fruit of the Spirit is... Patient Endurance, Kindness, Generosity...."

When I do what is right, or refuse to do what is wrong, do people sense that in me there is more to this than just ethical behavior or law observance? Do they get the feeling I am acting out of faithfulness to a personal relationship? That for me, "obedience" is faithfulness to a covenant, an experience of love? "The fruit of the Spirit is... Faithfulness...."

Do those I live and work with recognize in me an a priori abstinence from power? An abhorrence of getting things done by intellectual dominance, threats, or intimidation? Is my way the way of gentleness and persuasion? Always drawing rather than pushing? "The fruit of the Spirit is... Gentleness..."

And when I exercise self-control, does it come across to others as surrender? Instead of being impressed, or perhaps intimidated, by my "higher self"—my intellect and will—dominating my "lower self" of appetites and emotions, do they somehow sense that my whole self is surrendered to the control of another? Instead of a self-discipline that is rigid, off-putting, or even frightening to others, does my self-control make people feel safe, at ease with me, and welcome? The "fruit of the Spirit" is the Self-Control of total surrender to God.

We are not talking here about ordinary human virtues. These are not just character traits deliberately developed or culturally acquired. Human efforts play a part, of course, but they cannot explain the end product. To be a Christian is to be divine. The "grace of the Lord Jesus Christ" is "the favor of sharing in the divine life of God." Saint Paul's theme song is that those who are "in Christ Jesus" should live by "the law of the Spirit of life in Christ." This means we are called and empowered to live on the level of God. We "walk not according to the flesh"—human nature alone—"but according to the Spirit" (Romans 8:1ff.).

> If we live by the Spirit, let us also be guided by the Spirit....
> If you are led by the Spirit, you are not subject to the law.
> ■ GALATIANS 5:16, 25

As Christians, we don't evaluate our lives by the laws of good human morality—the Ten Commandments—but by the New Law of Christ, which is summarized, though not complete, in the Sermon on the Mount (Matthew, chapters 5 to 7).

Surprise! We can read the Sermon on the Mount from beginning to end, and we will not find a single rule! The New Law of Christ is not presented in the form of rules. It does not have the precision of concrete laws. Jesus presents it in the form of ideals to aim at: ideals that attempt to translate God's way of thinking and loving into various forms of human behavior.

A rule tells us what to do. An ideal tells us what to aim at. Rules are obligations. Ideals are invitations.

Rules are boundary markers—in Latin, *fines*. They mark out a determined path. Ideals—at least the divine ideals of the New Law—are *in-finite*, boundless in their scope. They simply point us in a direction. And there is no limit, no end, no *finis* to how far we can go. They launch us toward the infinite Truth, Goodness, Oneness, and Being (Life) of God himself.

When we live as good human beings, we keep within the channel markers of the Ten Commandments. When we live the divine life of God, we are loose on the open sea, guiding ourselves by a single star, Jesus.

Pope Saint John Paul II teaches this in *The Splendor of Truth* (no. 16):

> The Beatitudes [and all the exhortations in the Sermon on the Mount] are not specifically concerned with certain particular rules of behavior. Rather, they speak of basic attitudes and dispositions in life......In their originality and profundity they are a sort of "self-portrait of Christ," and for this very reason are invitations to discipleship [ongoing learning], and to communion of life [deepening personal relationship] with Christ.

Jesus prescribes principles, not practices.

A principle, according to Aristotle, is "that from which something begins." A law is that in which an inquiry about morality ends. We begin with principles and come up with laws. Laws spell out concrete practices. We can judge whether or not we have kept a law—for example, whether or not we have lied, stolen, or killed. But it is not always easy to judge whether or not we have correctly applied a principle. Principles lack the precision of laws.

For example, when Jesus says, "Love one another as I have loved you," that does not spell out anything concrete that we should do. It is a principle to apply. It is the starting point from which every decision about conduct should begin.

Furthermore, even though Jesus calls this his "new commandment" (John 15:9,12), it is not so much a law to obey as an ideal to aim at. To love as Jesus loves is impossible for mere human beings. Only God can love as Jesus loves. This commandment does not prescribe a human action but a divine endeavor. We will be judged, not by whether we have done it, but by whether we have tried to do it. It is a "law of the Spirit of life in Christ": a guideline for those called and empowered by "the grace of the Lord Jesus Christ" to live on the level of God.

The New Law of Christ is a collection of principles and ideals, of starting points and goals to aim at. It doesn't say very much that is definite about the concrete actions in between. So the best way to judge whether or not we are living by the law of divine Life is to ask whether or not the evidence of divine Life is visible in our behavior.

This means we should look for the fruits of the Spirit. They are the benchmarks that tell us whether or not we are living a truly Christian life. If the fruits of the Spirit are evident in our life, we will be the "aroma of Christ" in the world.

And for the world.

Let's look at them now.

The Aroma of
LOVE

As the Father has loved me, so I have loved you; abide in my love...
This is my commandment, that you love one another as I have
loved you. JOHN 15:9, 12

The first fruit of the Spirit is Love (Galatians 5:22). Love is the first sign that identifies authentic Christians. Not the profession of true doctrines, not the observance of good moral laws, but the fact our lives are characterized by love—divine Love.

> By this everyone will know that you are my disciples, if you have love for one another. ▪ JOHN 13:35

And for everyone else.

Our existence is an experience of God loving us. Others should experience our existence as God in us loving them: to be Christian is to "Live in love, as Christ loved us and gave himself up for us, a fragrant offering and sacrifice to God" (Ephesians 5:2).

We are called to be the "aroma of Christ...the fragrance that comes from knowing him" (2 Corinthians 2:14).

Whenever we make visible the mystery of "Christ in us" (Colossians 1:27), that is the effect and manifestation of the Spirit. The first "fruit of the Spirit" is Love. So the first work of a Christian is to make God's love visible on earth. But first we have to understand what God's love is.

SPECIALISTS IN LOVE

Christians should be experts on love. "God is love" (1 John 4:8, 16). So the more we know God, the more we should know about love.

The love God has for us is a matter of experience as well as faith: "We have *known* and we *believe* the love God has for us." We need to reflect on our experience and on our faith until it is obvious to us that we "abide in love and God abides in us" (see 1 John 4:16).

For example, something should come alive in us when the Mass begins: "May... the love of God... be with you." Awareness of the love we have experienced should flood our hearts.

But does it?

For many of us, our experience of God's love may have been blocked by a misleading focus on keeping the Commandments. We may have believed that God's love for us was conditional on our keeping the Commandments. After all, Jesus said: "If you keep my commandments, you will abide in my love, just as I have kept my Father's commandments and abide in his love" (John 15:10). That led some of us to keep the Commandments out of fear that if we didn't, God wouldn't love us.

Obeying God should be an experience of responding to the God who loves us unconditionally. But that is not always the case.

So let us look at how Christianity—that is, conscious relationship with the Father, Son, and Spirit through identification with Jesus Christ—empowers us to love as Jesus loved.

WHY ARE WE LOVABLE?

Before all else, Christianity assures us that we are loved by God and tells us why.

> In this is love, not that we loved God but that God loved
> us....Beloved, since God loved us so much, we also ought
> to love one another....We love because God first loved us.
> ▪ 1 JOHN 4:10–19

But why does God love us? Why does God love me? Why would anybody?

The Christian answer to this—and it is unique—is that God loves us because "God sees and loves in us what God sees and loves in Christ" (Preface VII in the Mass for Sundays of Ordinary Time, 1985 version).

When we were born of our parents, they passed on to us their human life. God saw us and loved us as little human babies, endowed with intellect and will, and therefore with the capacity to know God and love God as human beings.

But when we "became Christ" at baptism, God chose to add to this the gift of knowing him as he knows himself, divinely. God did this the only way he could, by letting us share in his own divine life by Grace: letting us share in his own divine act of knowing by the gift of Faith, and in his own divine act of loving by the gift of Love. This was a new, a second birth (John 3:5).

God did this by incorporating us into the body of Jesus, Son of the divine Father, and Son of Mary, a human mother. Jesus is both human and divine. And "in Christ" God sees us also as both human and divine—not divine by nature, as Jesus is, but by sharing in the life and nature of God as members of Christ's body. The mystery of our Christian existence is that by baptism we "became Christ." And that is how the Father sees us.

The words are those of St. Augustine:

> Let us rejoice then and give thanks that we have become
> not only Christians, but Christ himself. Do you understand
> and grasp, brethren, God's grace toward us? Marvel and
> rejoice: we have *become Christ*. ▪ QUOTED IN THE CATECHISM
> OF THE CATHOLIC CHURCH, 795

That means that by Grace we have the good qualities—the lovable characteristics—of Jesus himself. And God sees them in us.

"God sees and loves in us what God sees and loves in Christ."

> For those whom God foreknew, God also predestined to
> be conformed to the image of God's Son, in order that he
> might be the firstborn within a large family. ▪ ROMANS 8:29

Even if we are not making as much use of the gifts of the Spirit, or revealing as much of the fruits of the Spirit as we ought to, we still have them. God sees them in us.

By the gift of divine Faith we share in Christ's own divine act of knowing. God loves us because we think like Jesus does. Through the Holy Spirit and the gift of Understanding, we have the "mind of Christ" (see 1 Corinthians 2:9–16). We and Jesus are kindred spirits. Literally.

By the gift of divine love, Jesus lets us share in his own divine act of loving. God loves us because we love what Jesus loves. We have the heart of Christ.

We love the Father as Jesus does, as the Father's own sons and daughters:

> Because we are children, God has sent the Spirit of his Son
> into our hearts, crying, "Abba! Father!"…When we cry,
> "Abba! Father!" it is that very Spirit bearing witness with
> our spirit that we are children of God.
>
> ▪ GALATIANS 4:6; ROMANS 8:15

The Father also loves us because we love Jesus: "The Father himself loves you, because you have loved me and have believed that I came from God" (John 16:27).

We love Jesus as our brother, because his Father is our Father—and because we have the gift of the Holy Spirit called "Piety," which is the "gut bond" of Loyalty to family and friends. Jesus was explicit about our relationship:

"Who is my mother, and who are my brothers?" And pointing to his disciples, he said, "Here are my mother and my brothers!....My mother and my brothers are those who hear the word of God and do it."..."Go to my brothers and say to them, 'I am ascending to my Father and your Father, to my God and your God.'" ▪ MATTHEW 12:48; JOHN 20:17

The one who sanctifies and those who are sanctified all have one Father. For this reason Jesus is not ashamed to call them brothers and sisters. ▪ HEBREWS 2:11

In the same way, we love as brothers and sisters all who are "in Christ," or called to be, whether consciously Christians or not. They are our family.

Now concerning love of the brothers and sisters, you do not need to have anyone write to you, for you yourselves have been taught by God to love one another; and indeed you do love all the brothers and sisters....But we urge you, beloved, to do so more and more. ▪ 1 THESSALONIANS 4:9–10

By the gift of Awe (Fear) of the Lord, we know God as God, and ourselves as nothingness called into existence and receiving existence right now only by God's free, continuing choice. This is humility. And it makes us lovable to God.

What does the LORD require of you but to do justice, love kindness, and walk humbly with your God?....All these things my hand has made....This is the one whom I esteem: the humble and contrite in spirit, who trembles at my word. ▪ MICAH 6:8; ISAIAH 66:2

God has also given us divine Hope, and the gift of Wisdom, by which we constantly look to and long for our "last end": total union of mind and heart and will with God forever. That is "eternal Life." Because we have set our hearts on the same goal, and accepted the same ideals as Jesus, opening ourselves to all that is True and Good and Beautiful, God loves us.

> And this is eternal Life, that they may know you, the only true God, and Jesus Christ whom you have sent....Those who love their life lose it, and those who hate their life in this world will keep it for eternal Life.
> ▪ JOHN 6:40, 12:25; 17:3

> My child, if your heart is wise, my heart too will be glad.
> ▪ PROVERBS 23:15

The point is, all that we have by Grace and the gifts of the Holy Spirit are our own good qualities. They are us. They are what we are. God loves us because we are like Jesus.

These are gifts of God, but they are given to us. They are part of our being, of who we are. The same good qualities God sees in Jesus, God sees in us. And God loves us for them.

Of course, we don't have those qualities in the same measure that Jesus does. Christ is still growing to "full stature" in us and we in him:

> The gifts he gave were...for building up the body of Christ, until all of us come to...maturity, to the measure of the full stature of Christ....We must grow up in every way into him who is the head, into Christ...who, as each part is working properly, promotes the body's growth in building itself up in love. ▪ EPHESIANS 4:13–16

The good qualities of Jesus that God sees in us are not yet perfect; they are still developing. But they are there. They are *our* good qualities. And God loves us because God recognizes them in us, the way a parent recognizes good qualities in a child that has not yet fully developed. God sees what we are and wants us to *esse et bene esse*: "to be and to become all we can be" (Saint Augustine's definition of love).

That is what the New Law of Christ incites us to do.

Paul summed it up: "It is no longer I who live, but it is Christ who lives in me" (Galatians 2:20). We have "become Christ." God "sees and loves in us what God sees and loves in Christ."

HOW DO WE DO THIS?

If we are going to be the "aroma of Christ" in the world, and to all around us, we need to bring all this down to ground level and put it to the test of daily experience.

On a day-to-day basis, how does my life show the fruit of love? Here are some questions to ask:

- When I wake up in the morning, do I remind myself that I am getting up to love?
- When I sit down to breakfast, am I more intent on eating or on showing love for those present?
- When I go to work, am I conscious that showing love is the first item on my job description? Do I give it priority over everything else? Do I consciously try to be loving to everyone?
- Do I try to make all of my business decisions profit others as well as myself? Can I say that in all of them I am loving my neighbor as myself? Loving others as Jesus loves me?
- Do I discriminate against anyone? Treat anyone as less important than anyone else? Do I show the same respect to the janitor that I show to my boss?

- If I am the boss, do I insist that all show the same respect to each other that they show to me?
- Do I consciously deal with everyone the way I would with my brother or sister?
- Do I praise coworkers and other people every chance I get? Do I smile at everyone? Say hello?
- Am I more consistent in expressing love for my children than in correcting them?
- In my thoughts, as well as in my words, do I always balance off criticism of others with understanding, sympathy, and recognition of their good points?
- When someone does wrong, is my first reaction concern for the wrongdoer, as it would be for one of my children, or is it to see justice done? Do I want justice with mercy, or simply justice?
- To "do unto others as I would have them do unto me," do I share with others the truth I know? My faith? My experiences of God? The hope that keeps me going?
- Do I fulfill all of my religious obligations, not as "obligations" but as loving, personal responses to Jesus and to the Father, in conscious union with the Holy Spirit?
- For me, are laws just ways to love? And is love my all-encompassing law?
- Do I know that God loves me? Do I understand why?
- Do I understand why Jesus loves others? Do I try to love them in the same way?

The Aroma of
JOY

"I have told you this so that my joy might be in you and your joy might be complete." JOHN 15:11

The second fruit of the Spirit is Joy.

It is a common saying among Christians that "joy is the infallible sign of the presence of God." We say, "A sad Christian is a sad Christian indeed."

That is logical. If the second "fruit of the Spirit" is Joy, it follows that people who are living by the Spirit should experience Joy, and it should be visible in their lives.

For Christians, Joy and suffering are compatible. The ultimate proof of this is Jesus himself, who had deep Joy—not to be confused with superficial feelings of joy—even while suffering on the cross. His Joy came from the consciousness that through his suffering he was bringing about what he came to earth to do: "I came that they might have life, and have it to the full" (John 10:10). He found his Joy in loving, and no amount of pain could prevail against it. Something like a woman giving birth:

> "Very truly, I tell you, you will weep and mourn, but the world will rejoice; you will have pain, but your pain will turn into Joy. When a woman is in labor, she has pain, because her hour has come. But when her child is born, she no longer remembers the anguish because of the joy of having brought a human being into the world." ▪ JOHN 16:20-21

Christianity is very different from Buddhism. Buddhism was inspired by an awareness of human suffering and a desire to find a path of spiritual practices by which one might deal with suffering, draw its teeth, and eventually escape from suffering entirely. The focus of Christianity is not on suffering but on love. Christians are moved by love to alleviate the sufferings of others and to eradicate the causes of suffering in the world, but that is a consequence of Christianity, not its goal. The goal of Christianity is deep, all embracing, total union with God and others in mind and heart and will—not a union that can be achieved by any human practices, but one made possible for us by the free gift of "Grace," the favor of sharing in God's own divine Life. If we have this gift, then whether we are suffering or not, we can have Joy.

Christians live for what Paul prayed for:

> I pray that you may have the power to comprehend, with
> all the saints, what is the breadth and length and height and
> depth, and to know the love of Christ that surpasses knowl-
> edge, so that you may be filled with all the fullness of God.
>
> ▪ EPHESIANS 3:18–19

Christian Joy is based, not on negation, but on affirmation; not on escaping, but on embracing. Christians have Joy, not because we have found a way to ignore pain, but because we have found something else. We know the Good News.

Our Joy depends on memory, on keeping aware of the Good News. And believing it. Christian Joy is the fruit and proof of the gift of divine Faith, enhanced by the gift of the Holy Spirit called Understanding.

Paul prays that we will "comprehend" and "know" the love of Christ. Jesus said we will find Joy by keeping aware of what he told us: "I have said these things to you so that my Joy may be in you, and that your Joy may be complete" (John 15:11).

If we are aware of the Good News, nothing can take away our Joy. If we are not aware of the Good News, nothing can give us joy that is lasting or complete.

What is the Good News?

It is the gospel.

The word comes from the Old English *gōdspel*, from *gōd* "good," and *spel* "news, a story." Christianity is based on the good news, the story, of Jesus Christ. As long as we are aware of that story, we have a reason for Joy.

Christian Joy is dependent on remembering. Whenever we feel sad, depressed, or discouraged, we need to recall whatever we know that is a cause for happiness, enthusiasm, and encouragement. For example, no matter what we are experiencing here and now, we should make ourselves conscious that we have within us, right now, everything required to make us totally happy for all eternity. We are living right now by God's own Life. That is "the Grace of our Lord Jesus Christ" that we proclaim at the beginning of every Mass.

Suppose we feel unloved. And maybe we actually are unloved—by people. Then we recall that Jesus said, "As the Father has loved me, so I have loved you; abide in my love" (John 15:9). Is that not love enough to give anyone Joy? Again, we are invited in every Mass to remember the "love of God" the Father.

If we feel lonely, isolated, cut off from other people, the Mass reminds us that we have "communion in the Holy Spirit" with all the believers—our brothers and sisters—throughout the world.

Suppose we feel like failures. And perhaps we really are failing in everything we do. Then we remember that Jesus said, "I am the vine, you are the branches. Those who abide in me and I in them bear much fruit, because apart from me you can do nothing.... You did not choose me but I chose you. And I appointed you to go and bear fruit, fruit that will last" (John 15:5, 16).

Success and failure do not depend on visible results in this world. In fact, anything done "apart from" Jesus is "nothing," no matter how impressive it may seem. But if we are "abiding in him," we are certain that we are bearing fruit, because he says we are. We take it on faith, which is the most certain kind of knowledge. That is cause for Joy.

Suppose we are sad because we have lost loved ones in death. When Jesus was about to die, he told his beloved disciples, "A little while, and you will no longer see me, and again a little while, and you will see me....You will weep and mourn...but your pain will turn into Joy....I will see you again, and your hearts will rejoice, and no one will take your Joy from you" (John 16:17–22).

He says the same to us about the loss we feel for those who have gone ahead of us into total union with God. Jesus does not deny the pain of mourning a loved one. He himself wept at the tomb of Lazarus. But he adds something. He says, "You will see each other again, your pain will turn into joy." He doesn't say not to mourn. He says, "Blessed are those who mourn, for they will be comforted" (Matthew 5:4).

Death is not the final word.

Suppose we are broke, have lost our job, the bank is foreclosing on our house, and we have nowhere to go. We remember Jesus said, "I tell you, do not worry about your life...saying, 'What will we eat?' or 'What will we drink?' or 'What will we wear?'....Your heavenly Father knows that you need all these things...So do not worry about tomorrow" (Matthew 6:25–34).

How can we be sad, just because we are broke? Our Father is rich. All we have to do is keep doing what we can do and wait for the Father to come through with what we need.

Even the fear of death cannot take away our Joy. Jesus said, "Do not fear those who kill the body but cannot kill the soul....Are not two sparrows sold for a penny? Yet not one of them will fall to the ground apart from your Father....So do not be afraid; you are of more value than many sparrows" (Matthew 10:28–29).

Notice that in none of these passages does Jesus deny that the suffering exists. He calls our attention to something else, something added, that puts our pain into perspective and gives us cause for Joy. It is a Joy that depends on Hope.

> May the God of Hope fill you with all Joy and Peace in
> believing, so that you may abound in Hope by the power of
> the Holy Spirit. ▪ ROMANS 15:13

Joy is a fruit of the Spirit. After telling us, "I have said these things to you so that my Joy may be in you, and that your Joy may be complete" (John 15:11), he promised that the Spirit would remind us of the Good News:

> The Advocate, the Holy Spirit, whom the Father will send
> in my name, will teach you everything, and remind you of
> all that I have said to you. ▪ JOHN 14:26

When as Christians we are aware of "all that he has said," we experience Joy. And our Joy will surround us like an aura. We will be the *aroma of Christ* in the world, the *fragrance that comes from knowing him.*

HOW DO WE DO THIS?
If we are going to be the "aroma of Christ" in the world, and to all around us, we need to bring all this down to ground level and put it to the test of daily experience.

- Would most people who know me call me a joyful person?
- Would I say I experience Joy most of the time—at least, when I stop to reflect?
- Aside from temporary disturbances, is there anything deep and abiding that diminishes my joy?

- If so, is there anything I can do about it that I am not already doing?
- Do I know how to find Joy in Christ when there is suffering in my life? When I am frustrated? Do I know what to remember? Do I go there?
- If I made a list of the things that take away my joy, could I match each one with something from the gospels that gives me Joy in spite of them?
- When I am not feeling human joy, do I make sure, without hiding my pain, that my words and body language express the underlying divine Joy that depends on faith instead of on feelings—so that I spread the "aroma of Christ" all around me?

The Aroma of
PEACE

*"Peace I give to you… Do not let your hearts
be troubled, and do not let them be afraid."*

JOHN 14:27

J esus follows his promise of Joy immediately with the
promise of Peace. Christian Peace is the fruit and proof of
the gift of divine Hope.

Seek peace and pursue it ….Always be ready to make your
defense to anyone who demands from you an accounting
for the Hope that is in you. ▪ 1 PETER 3:11–15

When a Christian is part of a group, everyone should feel a calm-
ing influence. Whatever is going wrong, Christians know there
is something better we can look forward to with confidence. The
Good News is giving a new dimension to life on earth. We have
Hope.

Saint Paul summed up the Good News in three words: *"Christ
in you."* And he added, *"the hope of glory"* (Colossians 1:27). To
live and give Peace, what more do we need?

Where we are, Jesus is. Where Jesus is, there is the hope of
glory, and there should be the aura of Peace.

NOT PEACE BUT *PEACE*

Jesus is not talking about peace as the "absence of conflict," Jesus doesn't promise that.

> Do you think that I have come to bring peace to the earth? No, I tell you, but rather division! From now on five in one household will be divided, three against two and two against three; they will be divided: father against son and son against father, mother against daughter and daughter against mother.... ▪ LUKE 12:51–53

The peace Jesus promises is the Peace that is the fruit of the Spirit. That Peace is a mystery. It is the mystery of appreciated oneness with God, and oneness with each other "in Christ"—the Peace of relationship. Ultimately, it is the Peace the Father, Son, and Spirit find in their relationship with each other, the Peace we will experience when are perfectly united with God and each other around one table at the "wedding banquet of the Lamb."

This is the "hope of glory." Jesus prayed, "Holy Father, protect those you have given me....The glory you have given me I have given them, so that they may be one, as we are one, I in them and you in me...so that the world may know that you have sent me and have loved them even as you have loved me" (see John 17:11–23).

Peace depends on being conscious of Hope: our hope of being totally One—with God, with others, and with our own selves— in the glory of the "wedding banquet of the Lamb."

The fruit of the Spirit is an interior Peace. But it should be noticeable, like an aura. All who know Jesus should be surrounded with "the fragrance that comes from knowing him." For we are "the aroma of Christ" in the world.

CHRIST'S PEACE IS A MYSTERY

Christ's Peace is "the Peace of God, which surpasses all understanding" (Philippians 4:7). It is experienced only by those who share in the divine Life of God, which is the definition of "Grace." It is the fruit—and also the preservative—of union with God. Paul says this Peace "will stand guard over your hearts and your minds in Christ Jesus" (Philippians 4:7).

HOW DO WE EXPERIENCE PEACE?

For Peace we must first experience within ourselves the oneness of unified desire. Jesus said: "Strive first for the kingdom of God and his righteousness, and all these things will be given to you as well" (Matthew 6:33). If we make it our goal in life to seek happiness through relationship with God, we will not be torn in different directions. Focus will give us peace.

And we will never be frustrated, never have a valid reason for discouragement. We will have the peace of satisfiable desire. Jesus told Martha when she was "worried and distracted by many things" that "there is need of only one thing" (Luke 10:41)—to remain conscious of the nearness of God, united to God in mind and heart and desire.

This is the essence, the ultimate Truth and Goodness of Christianity: we are One with the Father, Son, and Holy Spirit in sharing the divine Life that is their Being. Eternal Life. "And this is eternal Life, that they may know you, the only true God, and Jesus Christ whom you have sent" (John 6:40; 12:25; 17:3).

Obviously, we are not simply God. Our life, our being, had a beginning. We are not eternal by nature. We only "share" in the Life of God. By human nature we are what we are: limited, "finite" creatures whose life, whose existence, began in a moment of time. But by "Grace," God is sharing with us, making us partakers of, God's own eternal, infinite Life and Existence. We share in God's Being as God. This is the "Grace—the word means 'favor,' 'gift'—

of the Lord Jesus Christ." And this gift is what the early Christians saw as "salvation" and wished for each other most often when they greeted one another.

Seventeen times "Grace" and "Peace" are joined together in the New Testament as a greeting. Obviously, in the early Church, one implied the other.

> To all God's beloved in Rome, who are called to be saints:
> Grace to you and Peace from God our Father and the Lord
> Jesus Christ. ▪ ROMANS 1:7

The phrase "Grace and Peace" is repeated in 1 Corinthians 1:3; 2 Corinthians 1:2; Galatians 1:3; Ephesians 1:2; Philippians 1:2; Colossians 1:2; 2 Thessalonians 1:2; 1 Timothy 1:2; 2 Timothy 1:2; Titus 1:4; Philemon 3; 1 Peter 1:2; 2 Peter 1:2; 2 John 3; Revelation 1:4.

"The Grace of our Lord Jesus Christ" is the foundation, the essence, and the core of our Peace. No matter what disturbs us, we find Peace in the realization that we have within us, right now, everything required to make us totally happy for all eternity.

And what is that? It is Oneness with God. We are One with the Father, Son, and Spirit, One with them as they are One with each other. That is what Jesus asked for his disciples:

> "...that they may all be One. As you, Father, are in me
> and I am in you, may they also be in us...that they may be
> One, as we are one, I in them and you in me, that they may
> become completely One." ▪ JOHN 17:20–23

In heaven, everyone "rests in peace," because everyone is in possession of the All that is God: all Truth, all Goodness, all Life and Being. But already on earth, those who share in the Life (Being) of God by Grace have access to all Truth by the light of Faith, are assured of all Good by the gift of Hope, and experience the Oneness of God in the love that "binds everything together in perfect harmony, [so that] the Peace of Christ [rules] in your hearts, to which indeed you were called in the one body" (Colossians 3:14–15).

This is "the Grace of our Lord Jesus Christ." It frees us from what most commonly disturbs our peace on this earth: worry, confusion, guilt, and fear.

FREEDOM FROM WORRY

Christians know that God is not just our Creator; God is our Father. The Father is giving us existence—not just as human beings, but as his own children. Because we are reborn "of water and the Spirit" (John 3:5), we live by the Life of our Father, the divine Life of God. We are God's true-born sons and daughters, with the right to call God "Father." We have the Peace of knowing the Father cares for us and takes care of us as our Father. Jesus said it:

> "Therefore I tell you, do not worry about your life, what you will eat or what you will drink, or about your body, what you will wear. Is not life more than food, and the body more than clothing? Look at the birds of the air; they neither sow nor reap nor gather into barns, and yet your heavenly Father feeds them. Are you not of more value than they? ... Therefore do not worry about tomorrow, for tomorrow will worry about its own things. Sufficient for the day is its own trouble." ▪ MATTHEW 6:25–34

> "Can any of you by worrying add a single hour to your span of life? If then you are not able to do so small a thing as that, why do you worry about the rest? ... Do not keep worrying. For it is the [children of this world] that strive after all these things, and your Father knows that you need them.

Instead, strive for God's kingdom, and these things will be given to you as well." ▪ LUKE 12:25-31

Jesus says this. But we must choose to believe him. We only experience the Peace of freedom from worry when we consciously choose to put our trust in our Father. Those who trust in the relationship they have with God as Father make visible in their lives the fruit of Peace.

FREEDOM FROM CONFUSION

Sometimes our peace is troubled, not by concerns about our physical needs, but by questions that disturb our peace of mind. Jesus promises our Father will give us the answers we need:

> "Ask, and it will be given you; search, and you will find; knock, and the door will be opened for you....Is there anyone among you who, if your child asks for bread, will give a stone?...If you then...know how to give good gifts to your children, how much more will your Father in heaven give good things to those who ask him!"
> ▪ MATTHEW 7:7-11

Jesus said (Matthew 4:4): "It is written, 'One does not live by bread alone, but by every word that comes from the mouth of God.'" Our Father will never fail to give us his words, and his Spirit to help us understand them. If we keep knocking, searching, and believing, we will find.

Christians have the Peace of mind that comes from knowing where we come from, where we are going, and how to get there. The Father has given us Jesus as the Way, the Truth, and the Life (John 14:6; Luke 20:21). We have the answers to all the questions that matter. We know them, not just by reason, but by the divine gift of Faith. And Faith is the most certain form of knowledge. It is the gift of sharing in God's own act of knowing.

Knowing is an activity intrinsic to God's act of Being. It is part of God's Life. Because of this, the gift of Faith is the same in all who share in the Life of God by being "sons and daughters in the Son," living by the Life of Christ as members of his body on earth.

But the Truth is experienced, expressed, and made visible in different ways in the various members of Christ's body. The Truth of the Church is a shared truth, clarified by the insights of every individual member. "To each is given the manifestation of the Spirit for the common good" (1 Corinthians 12:7). The purpose is:

> to equip the saints for the work of ministry, for building up the Body of Christ, until all of us come to the unity of the Faith and of the knowledge of the Son of God, to maturity, to the measure of the full stature of Christ.
>
> ▪ EPHESIANS 4:12–13

In that unity is Peace:

> We must no longer be children, tossed to and fro and blown about by every wind of doctrine…but speaking the Truth in love, we must grow up in every way into him who is the head, into Christ…as each part, working properly, promotes the Body's growth in building itself up in love.
>
> ▪ EPHESIANS 4:14–16

Then "the Peace of God, which surpasses all understanding," will unite our hearts and our minds in Christ Jesus (Philippians 4:7).

This is the gift of the Father. Jesus promised it: "The Advocate, the Holy Spirit, whom the Father will send in my name, will teach you everything, and remind you of all that I have said to you" (John 14:26).

But we only experience the Peace of freedom from confusion when we consciously choose to believe the words of our Father. Those who are One with the Father in what they believe, and united with others in sharing it, make visible in their lives the fruit of Peace.

FREEDOM FROM GUILT

Sometimes our conscience disturbs our peace. Even the great St. Paul experienced this:

> I am of the flesh, sold into slavery under sin. I do not understand my own actions....For I do not do the good I want, but the evil I do not want....Wretched man that I am! Who will rescue me from this body of death? ▪ ROMANS 7:14–24

Paul knew the answer, of course. It is Jesus.

But Peace of conscience does not come from Jesus just forgiving our sins. It comes from Jesus who, as the Lamb of God, *takes away* our sins.

We have to insist on clarity here. God does not only forgive. Forgiveness does not change the one forgiven. Forgiveness alone does not give peace to those who must live with the memory of what they have done. The mystery of our redemption is that, through Jesus, our Father "was pleased to reconcile to himself all things...making Peace through the blood of his cross...so as to present us holy and blameless and irreproachable before him" (Colossians 1:20).

Christ gives Peace, not through an act of forgiveness, but through the "blood of his cross." He made us "holy and blameless and irreproachable," not by just forgiving us, but by dying so that we could die in him—and rise as a "new creation."

He did this by incorporating us, with all of our sins, into his body on the cross. Our sins became the sins of his own flesh. As

"Lamb of God," Jesus was made "to be sin, though he knew no sin, so that in him we might become the righteousness of God" (2 Corinthians 5:14–21; John 1:29).

Then he took us down into the grave with him so that we might die in him and rise in him as a "new creation." Now we are not just forgiven. We are innocent: "holy and blameless and irreproachable." Our sins went down into the grave with us when we died in Christ and were annihilated. The one who committed those sins died—and rose again in Christ as a "new creation," to be "holy and blameless and irreproachable before God" (2 Corinthians 5:17; Colossians 1:22).

> When you were dead in your sins...God made you alive together with him, having forgiven us all our sins, *erasing the record* that stood against us....God set this aside, nailing it to the cross. ▪ COLOSSIANS 2:13–14

We have the Peace of conscience we can only find by "becoming Christ."

> God, who is rich in mercy, out of the great love with which God loved us even when we were dead through our offenses, made us alive together with Christ—by Grace you have been saved—and raised us up with him and seated us with him in the heavenly places in Christ Jesus.
> ▪ EPHESIANS 2:1–6

> Therefore, since we are justified by Faith, we have Peace with God through our Lord Jesus Christ, through whom we have obtained access to this Grace in which we stand; and we boast in our Hope of sharing the glory of God.
> ▪ ROMANS 5:1–2

We "boast in our Hope." We don't claim to be perfect already. We still commit sins. But whenever, in the before-and-after time frame of our world, we repent of a sin newly committed, that sin is incorporated into the body of Jesus hanging on the cross at the center of time, in the eternal "now" of God. And it is annihilated in "the blood of the cross."

In God's time frame, where past, present, and future are all "now," we are already "raised up and seated with Christ in the heavenly places, holy and blameless and irreproachable in Christ Jesus, without a spot or wrinkle or anything of the kind, holy and without blemish"—provided, of course, that we "continue securely established and steadfast in the faith, without shifting from the Hope promised by the Gospel that we have heard" (see Ephesians 5:27; Colossians 1:23; 2 Peter 3:14).

We experience the Peace of freedom from guilt when we consciously choose to accept the mystery of dying with all of our sins and rising without any of them. Those who accept the mystery of this Oneness with Jesus in his death and rising make visible in their lives the fruit of Peace.

FREEDOM FROM FEAR

Jesus has freed us—totally—from the sins of our past. But we still fear the challenges we may face in the future. Aside from temptations to sin, we are afraid we won't be equal to the task entrusted to us, the mission of establishing the reign of God on earth.

But Jesus has told us not to fear:

> "Do not be afraid, little flock, for it is your Father's good
> pleasure to give you the kingdom." ▪ LUKE 12:32

> "I have said this to you, so that in me you may have Peace.
> In the world you face persecution. But take courage; I have
> conquered the world!" ▪ JOHN 16:33

"Peace I leave with you; my Peace I give to you. I do not give to you as the world gives. Do not let your hearts be troubled, and do not let them be afraid." ▪ JOHN 14:27

"Remember, I am with you always, to the end of the age."
▪ MATTHEW 28:20

Christians can keep trying to do the impossible without losing Peace, because by his resurrection Jesus has triumphed over the two greatest threats to human life: sin and death. We are afraid of nothing: "The law of the Spirit of Life in Christ Jesus has set us free from the law of sin and of death" (Romans 8:2). Now Jesus is "seated at the right hand of the power of God" (Luke 22:69). He has declared his Lordship:

"Peace be with you. As the Father has sent me, so I send you." When he had said this, he breathed on them and said to them, "Receive the Holy Spirit. If you forgive the sins of any, they are forgiven them; if you retain the sins of any, they are retained." ▪ JOHN 20:21–23

"All authority in heaven and on earth has been given to me. Go therefore and make disciples of all nations, baptizing them in the name of the Father and of the Son and of the Holy Spirit, and teaching them to obey everything that I have commanded you. And remember, I am with you always, to the end of the age." ▪ MATTHEW 28:18–20

We are not left to our own resources. Jesus, together with the Father, "has sent the Holy Spirit to us, as the first fruits of his life and death, to bring to perfection his work in the world and sanctify creation to the full" (Eucharistic Prayer IV, 1970 translation). He told his apostles: "I am sending upon you what my Father promised; so stay here in the city until you have been clothed with power from on high" (Luke 24:49).

The Church prays, "Send forth your Spirit, Lord, and our hearts will be regenerated. *And you will renew the face of the earth!*"

Because of this promise, Paul can encourage us: "May the God of Hope fill you with all Joy and Peace in believing, so that you may abound in Hope by the power of the Holy Spirit."

> I pray that … with the eyes of your heart enlightened, you
> may know what is the Hope to which God has called you
> and what is the immeasurable greatness of God's power
> for us who believe, according to the working of God's great
> power.
>
> God put this power to work in Christ when God raised
> him from the dead and seated him at God's right hand in
> the heavenly places, far above all rule and authority and
> power and dominion, and above every name that is named,
> not only in this age but also in the age to come. And God
> has put all things under his feet and has made him the head
> over all things for the Church, which is his Body, the full-
> ness of him who fills all in all. ▪ EPHESIANS 1:17–23

That is the foundation of the Peace that lets Christians dream "the impossible dream."

HOW DO WE DO THIS?

If we are going to be the "aroma of Christ" in the world, and to all around us, we need to bring all this down to ground level and put it to the test of daily experience. So each of us asks:

- Do I have an abiding peace in my heart? Am I conscious of a deep place in me like that of the depths of the ocean, where surface storms cannot cause disturbance? Do I withdraw into this place when the winds and waves of this life are distracting me?
- Where is my "anchor hold"—the place where I can go to find peace? How often do I use it?
- What do I worry about most often? What am I forgetting when I do?
- Am I "worried and distracted by many things"? Have I consciously, personally, decided "there is need of only one thing" (see Luke 10:40)? What is that?
- Deep down, do I really trust God to do everything Jesus promises?
- When I am about to go into a tense situation, do I remember to say the "WIT" prayer: "Lord, do this *with* me, do this *in* me, do this *through* me"?
- Is there any one thing that consistently disturbs my peace? Have I looked at it in the light of Scripture? Have I sought spiritual advice?
- When I know I am right and others are wrong, am I more inclined to seek common ground through dialogue or to prove my point through argument?
- Wherever I am, do I bring an atmosphere of peace that is the "aroma of Christ"? If not, what can I do about that?

The Church

BLESSED VISION OF PEACE

Rejoice greatly, O daughter Zion! Shout aloud,
O daughter Jerusalem! Your king comes to you;
triumphant and victorious... .He shall command
peace to the nations; his dominion shall be from sea
to sea, and from the River to the ends of the earth.
ZECHARIAH 9:9–10

T he Peace that is the fruit of the Spirit is not just the Peace of individual Christians. It is also a communal Peace. The Peace of Christ is a mystery of Oneness with God and with all of creation in God who alone is All. We experience this mystery, and the Peace it gives, most fully in the community—the "common unity"—of the Church.

Jesus prayed:

> "The glory that you have given me I have given them, so
> that they may be One, as we are One, I in them and you
> in me, that they may become completely One, so that the
> world may know that you have sent me and have loved
> them even as you have loved me." ▪ JOHN 17:20–24

Jesus counts on the Peace and Unity visible in his Church to draw the world to him.

This Unity is not just sociological: a grouping of people professing the same religious beliefs and committed to the same principles and practices who gather to worship together. It is not just based on human relationships. It is based on the relationship between the Father, Son, and Spirit, which allows them to be perfectly distinct as Persons yet perfectly one in their Life and Being as God.

This unity is mirrored in the Church as the Body of Christ on earth, where all of the members are distinct as persons endowed with a "variety of gifts and services," but are nevertheless only one body, living by the life of Christ and "activated by one and the same Spirit," so that "there may be no dissension within the body, but the members may have the same care for one another" (1 Corinthians 12).

When Jesus prayed "that they may all be One," he specified: "*As you, Father, are in me and I am in you*, may they also be in us" (John 17:21). This is Oneness on the level of mystery, the mystery of the Trinity itself: the incomprehensible and inexpressible Oneness of the Father, Son, and Spirit.

The Church needs to make visible the Peace that is the fruit of this Oneness.

THE TOWER OF BABEL

The story of the Tower of Babel (Genesis 11:1–9) was God's answer to the question children ask their parents: "Why doesn't everybody speak the same language we do?" God answered that in the beginning, "the whole world spoke the same language." Then humans discovered how to bake bricks. This made tall buildings possible. It went to their head. They decided to build a tower "with its top in the sky" and so "make a name for themselves." Technology is good, but it can come from ambition and lead to pride.

People motivated by pride and ambition are bound to fight. When this happened at Babel, to keep them from killing each other, God "confused the language" of those building the tower, and made it impossible for them to communicate. Then they had to separate. They split into different nations, and each developed its own language.

The result is a fragmented world. Human beings are divided in multiple ways: by culture, race, religion, nationality, social class, political preferences, etc. And, within every one of these categories, they are further divided by innumerable differences of opinion and orientation. Frequently, they are unable to communicate with each other. Although they use the same words, they just "don't speak the same language."

That is what the story of the Tower of Babel is all about.

It is still happening. While a missionary in Africa, I noticed a new mud hut outside a village. Asking about it, I was told, "That family did not get along with the chief. They moved out." A few months later there were a dozen new huts. Then there were none. I was told, "A lot of people didn't get along with the chief, so more moved out. When there were enough of them, they moved away and started a new village." In a country without writing, it would only be a matter of time before they were speaking a different dialect, then a different language.

Even people who live in the same city, if they move in separate circles, without fruitful social contact, soon cannot communicate with each other. Words like "justice," "equality," or "freedom" have different meanings for them—even the basic definitions of right and wrong.

If not, why did people have to take to the streets in 2020 protesting that "Black Lives Matter"?

Babel, or Babylon, near modern Baghdad, is named from the Hebrew *balal*, "to mix, confuse." The *Jerome Biblical Commentary* says this story is used "to give the theological reason for the division of the human race....The sin of our first parents resulted in the alienation of humans from God (3:22–24) and from their fellow humans (4:1–16). From sin now results the alienation of all human society from God and of humans from one another."

The story of Babel attributes this natural consequence to an act of God, as Scripture often does. But God did not really cause the discord. God's own action is always unifying. The prophets announced the future reversal of this alienation, and the prophecy was fulfilled on Pentecost, when the apostles preached to people of different tongues, gathered from different countries. By the power of the Holy Spirit "each one heard them speaking in the native language of each." This was a preview of the reversal of Babel, when all people will be One, speaking the "language of the Spirit" (see Isaiah 2:1–5; Acts 2:1–17).

This is the meaning of the "gift of tongues" that people experienced at Pentecost.

Ironically, the builders of Babel thought their technology would protect them from being "scattered all over the earth." But their effort to protect themselves and their society from dissolution without submission to God had the opposite effect. Ultimately, the only way the human race will ever live in peace is through union with Jesus Christ, who said, "Whoever does not gather with me scatters" (Matthew 12:30). God's "plan for the fullness of time" is to "gather up all things in Christ, things in heaven and things on earth." God does it, not by force, but by offering God's own self to us in love. We must do likewise. "Happy the people the Lord has chosen to be God's own" (Matthew 12:30; Ephesians 1:10; 2:13–14. And see the October 3, 2020 encyclical of Pope Francis, *Fratelli Tutti*, published too late to be adequately quoted when this book was written).

DIVISION WITHIN THE CHURCH

We have to face the fact that in our day there are divisions in the Church itself. Every peer group speaks the special "language" of its culture, which both defines and distorts truth, restricting our ability to understand other people and even the word of God.

God's answer to all this is to pour out his Spirit on the "prophets." These are believers who accept their baptismal consecration as prophets and stand up in the power of the "gift of the Spirit" to challenge the assumptions of their culture, including the unexamined teachings and practices of "cultural Christianity" that the Second Vatican Council urged "all concerned to remove or correct" in the measure that they are abusive, excessive or defective (see the *Constitution on the Church*, 51; and the *Constitution on the Church in Modern World*, 19).

Prophets disturb false peace for the sake of establishing true Peace. Sometimes this brings them into conflict with the "priests"—seen as the guardians of orthodoxy, law, and order. The "prophets" open us to the future, while the "priests" keep us faithful to the past. Both roles are necessary.

The two most common—and misleading—labels that divide us today are "conservative" and "liberal." The "liberals" cause division by calling for change, the "conservatives" by resisting it. How do we keep them both from dividing us and destroying the Peace of the Church?

Jesus said: "Every scribe who has been trained for the kingdom of heaven is like the master of a household who brings out of his treasure what is new and what is old" (Matthew 13:52).

First, we have to remember that the Peace of Christ is not the absence of conflict (Luke 12:51). In fact, Francis, the Bishop of Rome, made the shocking statement that the Holy Spirit "creates...differences among the churches, almost as if he were an Apostle of Babel!"

"Babel" stands for division. Francis, shockingly, sees the Holy Spirit causing division in the Church by giving different charisms and inspiring prophetic innovations.

"But, on the other hand," he continues, "it is also the Holy Spirit who creates unity from these differences, not in 'equality' [total sameness, uniformity] but in harmony.... The Paraclete, who gives different charisms to each, unites us in this community of the Church that worships [the unity amid diversity of] the Father, the Son, and Holy Spirit" (Andrea Tornielli, *Francis: Pope of a New World*).

We need to bear in mind that those singing in "harmony" are, by definition, not all singing the same note.

Francis explains the working of the Spirit:

> First...the Spirit generates diversity, for in every age the Spirit causes new and varied charisms to blossom. Then the Spirit brings about unity: the Spirit joins together, gathers and restores harmony... a union that is not uniformity, but *unity in diversity*.
>
> For this to happen, we need to avoid two recurrent temptations. The first temptation seeks diversity without unity. This happens when we want to separate, when we take sides and form parties, when we adopt rigid and airtight positions, when we become locked into our own ideas and ways of doing things, perhaps even thinking that we are better than others, or always in the right, when we become so-called "guardians of the truth." When this happens, we

choose the part over the whole, belonging to this or that group before belonging to the Church. We become avid supporters of one side, rather than brothers and sisters in the one Spirit. We become Christians of the "right" or the "left," before being on the side of Jesus, unbending guardians of the past or the avant-garde of the future before being humble and grateful children of the Church. The result is diversity without unity.

The opposite temptation is that of seeking unity without diversity. Here, unity becomes uniformity, where everyone has to do everything together and in the same way, always thinking alike. Unity ends up being homogeneity and no longer freedom. But, as Saint Paul says, "where the Spirit of the Lord is, there is freedom" (2 Corinthians 3:17).

So the prayer we make to the Holy Spirit is … for a heart that feels that the Church is our Mother and our home, an open and welcoming home where the manifold Joy of the Holy Spirit is shared.

▪ HOMILY FOR PENTECOST SUNDAY, JUNE 4, 2017

The characteristic of the Spirit is that the Spirit "blows where it chooses." You "hear the sound of it, but you do not know where it comes from or where it goes. So it is with everyone who is born of the Spirit." Christian behavior by definition is unpredictable. The "prophets" are full of surprises (John 3:5–8).

In the human Jesus, and in his human body on earth, the Spirit responds to the changing conditions of time and place and culture. Unlike the Pharisees, Christians do not recognize each other through a predictable uniformity of rules and rites and customs but in the recognized harmony of unpredictable actions inspired by the Holy Spirit according to the changing circumstances of time and culture in every people and part of the world. This is what it means to be "catholic."

Unity in diversity. Uniformity is not catholic; it is not
Christian.... It is curious! What makes for diversity is the
same as what then makes for unity: the Holy Spirit....
Unity is not...to do by obligation everything together, or
think in the same way, or lose one's identity. Unity in diversity is precisely the contrary; it is to recognize and accept
joyfully the different gifts that the Holy Spirit gives each
one and to put them at the service of all in the Church.

▪ FRANCIS: ADDRESS TO THE FRATERNITY OF CHARISMATIC
COMMUNITIES, OCTOBER 31, 2014

While still Archbishop of Buenos Aires, "Padre Jorge" Bergoglio
said: "Precisely because one remains [in the Church], precisely
if one is faithful, one changes. One does not remain faithful to
the letter, like the traditionalists or the fundamentalists. Fidelity
is always a change, a blossoming, a growth" (Tornielli, *Francis:
Pope of a New World*).

But where there is change, there is conflict.

DIALOGUE

The answer to conflict is dialogue.

Francis begs for it:

All wars, all struggles, all problems we face that are not
resolved, are due to a lack of dialogue....When there is a
problem, dialogue: this makes peace. ▪ POPE FRANCIS,
TO A GROUP OF JAPANESE STUDENTS, AUGUST 21, 2013

Dialogue is born from an attitude of respect for the other
person, from a conviction that the other person has something good to say. It assumes that there is room in the
heart for the person's point of view, opinion, or propos-
al....In order to dialogue, it is necessary to know how to

lower the defenses, open the doors of the house, and offer
human warmth. ▪ "ON HEAVEN AND EARTH,"
SUDAMERICANA, 2011

In the world, in societies, there is little peace because
dialogue is lacking. It is hard to come out of the narrow
horizon of one's interests and open oneself to a true
and sincere encounter. Peace needs a tenacious, patient,
strong, intelligent dialogue where nothing is lost. Dialogue
can defeat war. Dialogue makes people of different gen-
erations, who often ignore one another, live together. It
makes citizens of different ethnic provenance and different
convictions live together. Dialogue is the way of peace,
because dialogue fosters understanding, harmony, con-
cord, peace. Because of this, it is vital that it grow, that it
spread among people of every condition and conviction
as a network of peace that protects the world and the
weakest....We must dialogue, meet with one another to
establish in the world the culture of dialogue, the culture of encounter. ▪ INTERNATIONAL MEETING FOR PEACE,
SEPTEMBER 29, 2013

WE ARE ONE "IN CHRIST"

God enables this dialogue fundamentally, at our core, by making
us all one "in Christ." This is the mystery at the heart of Christian
Unity.

So he came and proclaimed Peace to you who were far off
and Peace to those who were near; for through him both of
us have access in one Spirit to the Father.

So then you are no longer strangers and aliens, but you
are citizens with the saints and also members of the household of God, built upon the foundation of the apostles and

prophets, with Christ Jesus himself as the cornerstone. In him the whole structure is joined together and grows into a holy temple in the Lord; in whom you also are built together spiritually into a dwelling place for God.

■ EPHESIANS 2:17–22

The mystery of our Oneness as Church is that we are one body, the Body of Christ, whose unity and diversity are both the work of his Spirit.

Now there are varieties of gifts, but the same Spirit.... To each is given the manifestation of the Spirit for the common good....

For just as the body is one and has many members...so it is with Christ. For in the one Spirit we were all baptized into one body...and we were all made to drink of one Spirit....We have gifts that differ according to the grace given to us. ■ 1 CORINTHIANS 12; ROMANS 12

Christians believe that the whole human race is called to be one body in Christ, and that we who are visibly his body now should work to draw in everyone else by showing the fruit of the Spirit that is "the blessed vision of Peace."

Baptism with water is the normal way to be incorporated into Christ's body. Jesus said, "No one can enter the kingdom of God without being born of water and Spirit" (John 3:5). But we accept as members of the body of Christ all who are baptized by water, blood, or desire (see *Catechism of the Catholic Church*, 1260).

In the early Church, in times of persecution, some converts were put to death and died as martyrs while still preparing for baptism. The Church declared they died as Christians, "baptized in their blood."

Others received the Holy Spirit before they were baptized with water.

> While Peter was still speaking, the Holy Spirit fell upon all who heard the word. The circumcised believers who had come with Peter were astounded that the gift of the Holy Spirit had been poured out even on the Gentiles....Then Peter said, "Can anyone withhold the water for baptizing these people who have received the Holy Spirit just as we have?" So he ordered them to be baptized in the name of Jesus Christ. ▪ ACTS 10:44–48

In their case, the "Spirit testified" that they had received the Grace of divine Life before being baptized with water. Christians call this "baptism of desire." We believe there are many "anonymous Christians" whose Faith is known to God alone (see Eucharistic Prayer IV). They surrendered to God in Faith, perhaps without ever having heard the name of Jesus.

Since the reality of any individual's Faith is known to God alone, in practice we assume that anyone we deal with has received "the Grace of the Lord Jesus Christ" (2 Corinthians 13:14) and is a member of his body. Others may not express the "mystery of Faith" in the same words we do, or embody it in the same human practices. But we look for signs that the same Spirit who animates us is animating them. And we dialogue, seeking a mutually recognized human understanding of the divine mystery that is our common Peace.

> Above all, clothe yourselves with love, which binds everything together in perfect harmony. And let the Peace of Christ rule in your hearts, to which indeed you were called in the one body. And be thankful. ▪ COLOSSIANS 3:14–15

SUMMARY: THREE IN ONE

Like the Father, Son, and Spirit, the Good, the True, and the One go together. So Christ's Peace requires Christians to be united to one another in three ways. All three were embodied in the lifestyle of the first Christian community.

The True: First, as *disciples,* the Christians embodied commitment to a communal pursuit of the Truth. With minds enlightened by the divine gift of Faith they "devoted themselves to the apostles' teaching and fellowship, the breaking of bread and the prayers." This fostered peace of mind in awareness of being One in a communal pursuit of Truth visibly affirmed.

The Good: Second, as *prophets,* they embodied in their lifestyle a collective orientation toward the Good proclaimed in the New Law of Jesus. With wills empowered by the divine gift of Hope in Christ's promises, "all who believed were together and had all things in common. They would sell their possessions and goods and distribute the proceeds to all, as any had need." This bore witness to visible detachment from the things of this world and attachment to the ideals and values of the Good News announced by Jesus. This fostered peace of mind in awareness of being One in a common adherence to the Good.

The One: Third, as *priests in the Priest,* through mutual ministry they embodied their desire to be One with God and each other. Harmony, to be experienced, must be expressed. In music, there is no harmony until the notes are played. In the Church, experienced harmony of heart depends on our giving *expression,* in physical words and gestures, to the invisible faith, hope, and love that lie hidden in our minds and wills and hearts. To give that expression is to minister as a *priest.* And so, with hearts warmed by the divine gift of love, they "spent much time together in the temple; they broke bread at home and ate their food with glad and generous hearts, praising God." This fostered peace of heart in awareness of being One in a common insistence on maintaining that unity of the Spirit amid the diverse expression of gifts that is a characteristic of the Beautiful (see 1 Corinthians 12:4ff.).

In the early Church, the visible evidence of oneness in Being through this threefold unity of mind and will and heart in pursuit of the True, the Good, and the One bore the fruit of Peace:

> And day by day the Lord added to their number those who were being saved. ▪ ACTS 2:47

STEWARDS OF THE KINGSHIP OF CHRIST

There is one more thing to add. In today's Church—and in today's world, where everyone has a voice in government, and our conscience has been awakened to the responsibility we all have to care for the planet and everyone on it—Christians need to make manifest another kind of unity. As *kings*, or "stewards of the kingship of Christ," consecrated in baptism to establish the reign of God over every area and activity of human life on earth, we need to be visibly committed to *work for change*.

We have to reveal that our hearts are communally inflamed with the love of neighbor that Jesus redefined in the story of the good Samaritan (Luke 10:27ff.):

> "Who, do you think, was a neighbor to the man who fell into the hands of the robbers?" The man answered, "The one who showed him mercy." Jesus said to him, "Go and do likewise."

The "neighbor" is anyone in need of mercy. The root meaning of "mercy" is "aid given to another out of a sense of *relationship*." But Christians see themselves related as brother or sister to everyone who is or is called to be a child of our Father in heaven. So for Christians, "neighbor" includes the whole human race.

A classic definition of "love" is to want people "to be and to become everything they can be": *esse et bene esse.* Christians extend that love to the whole of creation. As fellow creatures, we are in relationship with everything God made. As much as possible, we want everything to *be*—to continue in existence—and to develop into everything it can be.

God has not only made us stewards of "God's mysteries," and of "the manifold grace of God" (1 Corinthians 4:1; 1 Peter 4:10). God has made us the "stewards of creation" and "set us over the whole world in all its wonder," to "have dominion" and take responsibility for everything God has made (Genesis 1:26; see Sunday Preface V, Eucharistic Prayer IV).

This was emphatically proclaimed when Pope Francis issued his encyclical letter *Laudato Si'*—*On Care for Our Common Home* (May 2015). Francis invited everyone, and specifically the world's 1.2 billion Catholics, to respond to the ecological crisis. Our baptismal consecration as "kings," or responsible stewards of the kingship of Christ, calls us to echo his words that "the cry of the Earth and the cry of the poor cannot continue." See also what Francis writes about fraternity and social friendship in *Fratelli Tutti.* This is the voice of God in our time.

This is a call to a Oneness with all of creation that only hints at the full "mystery of God's will….that God set forth in Christ, as a plan for the fullness of time, to gather up all things in him, things in heaven and things on earth." For God has "put all things under his feet and has made him the head over all things for the Church, which is his Body, the fullness of him who fills all in all" (Ephesians 1:9–10).

The assurance that the whole Church is united in doing something about disorder and dividedness in the world fosters the Peace of heart that is found in collective effort to make the world and all those God loves One in Christ. The Kingdom of God is a Oneness "no eye has seen, nor ear heard, nor the human heart conceived" (1 Corinthians 2:9). It is the Beauty of the "unity amid variety" of all God's creation made One in the Unity and Peace of the "wedding banquet of the Lamb" (Revelation 19:6).

There, finally, all of creation will "rest in Peace."

HOW DO WE DO THIS?

If we are going to be the "aroma of Christ" in the world, and to all around us, we need to bring all this down to ground level and put it to the test of daily experience.

- Do all the Christians you know understand the following words in the same way: "obedience," "discipleship," "Christian witness," "ministry," "responsible Christian"? What do you think these words call you to do?
- What does visible, conscious, personal relationship with Jesus have to do with Christians' experience of their relationship with each other? Do you recognize people who, regardless of their professed religion, or lack of it, seem to be listening to the Holy Spirit?
- What is your reaction to change and to people who call for changes? Do you dialogue? Listen? Voice answers to questions and challenges? Seek more information about what is new to you?
- For you, what is the difference in a Christian community between uniformity and harmony?
- What gives you a greater sense of security in the Church: to see a predictable uniformity in the observance of rules and rites and customs, or to see a recognizable harmony in unpredictable actions that are responses to the changing circumstances of time and culture?
- When there is a problem, do you dialogue with respect, believing that the other person has something good to say?

- Would you say that in your parish or diocese there are visible efforts to establish what Francis calls "the culture of dialogue, the culture of encounter"?
- Where do you see in your parish or diocese the three activities that unified the first Christian community (Acts 2:42–47)? What different forms do they take?
  1. They devoted themselves to the apostles' teaching and fellowship, to the breaking of bread and the prayers....
  2. All who believed were together and had all things in common; they would sell their possessions and goods and distribute the proceeds to all, as any had need.
  3. Day by day, as they spent much time together in the temple, they broke bread at home and ate their food with glad and generous hearts, praising God and having the goodwill of all the people.
- How do you see your parish drawing people to the Church today as in the beginning, when "day by day the Lord added to their number those who were being saved"?
- When and how do you see the Christian community giving *expression*, in physical words and gestures, to the invisible faith, hope, and love in our minds and wills and hearts? Is it impressive?
- What signs do you see that today's Church has been awakened to the responsibility we all have to care for the planet and everyone on it—signs that show we are visibly committed to work for change in society?
- Have you read Pope Francis' prophetic encyclical letters *Laudato Si'—On Care for Our Common Home* and *Fratelli Tutti—On Fraternity and Social Friendship*? Have you studied them, discussed them with others, taken any action because of them?

PATIENT ENDURANCE, KINDNESS, GENEROSITY

"If anyone wants to sue you and take your coat, give your cloak as well." MATTHEW 5:40

The fourth, fifth, and sixth fruits of the Spirit are Patient Endurance, Kindness, and Generosity. They go together.

The first three fruits of the Spirit—Love, Joy, and Peace—are abiding states of soul, a constant aura that surrounds those in whom Jesus lives: "the fragrance that comes from knowing him."

But the next three—Patient Endurance, Kindness, and Generosity—even though they are part of one's character, reveal themselves mostly in responses to particular circumstances. And they support one another.

Christians should be outstanding for their "Patient Endurance"—of people, circumstances, and events.

Pope Francis, citing 1 Corinthians 13:4–7 in *The Joy of Love*, 92, clarifies the meaning of "Patient Endurance" (*makrothumia*):

Its meaning is clarified by the Greek translation of the Old Testament, where we read that God is "slow to anger" (Exodus 34:6; Numbers 14:18). It refers, then, to the quality of one who does not act on impulse and avoids giving offense... The Book of Wisdom (cf. 11:23; 12:2, 15-18)... extols God's restraint, as leaving open the possibility of repentance, yet insists on his power, as revealed in his acts of mercy. God's "patience," shown in his mercy towards sinners, is a sign of his real power.

Being patient does not mean letting ourselves be constantly mistreated, tolerating physical aggression or allowing other people to use us. We encounter problems whenever we think that relationships or people ought to be perfect, or when we put ourselves at the center and expect things to turn out our way. Then everything makes us impatient, everything makes us react aggressively. Unless we cultivate patience, we will always find excuses for responding angrily. We will end up incapable of living together, antisocial, unable to control our impulses, and our families will become battlegrounds.... Patience takes root when I recognize that other people also have a right to live in this world, just as they are. It does not matter if they hold me back, if they unsettle my plans, or annoy me by the way they act or think, or if they are not everything I want them to be. Love always has an aspect of deep compassion that leads to accepting the other person as part of this world, even when he or she acts differently than I would like.

What supports our patience with other people is an abiding inclination to Kindness (*chrestotes* from *chrestós*: "serviceable, good"). Francis, in *The Joy of Love*, 93-94, interprets this to mean a person who "shows goodness by deeds." Kindness is "love ever ready to be of assistance." This should be an enduring attitude in every Christian who lives by the Spirit.

The word ... is derived from *chrestós*: a good person, one who shows goodness by deeds ....Paul wants to make it clear that "patience" is not a completely passive attitude, but one accompanied by activity, by a dynamic and creative interaction with others. The word indicates that love benefits and helps others. For this reason it is translated as "kind," as love ever ready to be of assistance.

... Paul wants to stress that love is more than a mere feeling. Rather, it should be understood along the lines of the Hebrew verb "to love"; it is "to do good." As Saint Ignatius of Loyola said, "Love is shown more by deeds than by words" (*Spiritual Exercises*, "Contemplation to Attain Love"). It thus shows its fruitfulness and allows us to experience the happiness of giving, the nobility and grandeur of spending ourselves unstintingly, without asking to be repaid, purely for the pleasure of giving and serving.

Christians get up in the morning to be kind. We spend our day being kind to others. Our focus is on what we can do for others, not on what others are doing for us—or to us. So when anyone wrongs us, imposes on us, or annoys us in any way, our immediate reaction—which really is a trained response—is to be kind. Kindness is "love ever ready to be of assistance." So when something goes wrong, or someone is having a bad day and drawing us into it, our first reaction is, "how can I help?" That Kindness is the visible expression of Patient Endurance.

Jesus gives three examples of what we have to endure from other people. But in every example he does not stop with Patient Endurance. Or even with responsive Kindness. In every case, he tells us to respond with Generosity (from *agathourgeo*, to "do good").

"I say to you, do not resist an evildoer. But if anyone strikes you on the right cheek, turn the other also; and if anyone

wants to sue you and take your coat, give your cloak as
well; and if anyone forces you to go one mile, go also the
second mile." ▪ MATTHEW 5:39–41

In every example Jesus gives here, the response to wrongdoing
is not just to endure with Patience; and not just to respond with
Kindness. It is to respond with overwhelming goodness: to be
extraordinarily Generous.

To "do good" like this, we have to remember that "the Grace
of the Lord Jesus Christ" is the favor of sharing in the divine Life
of God. And God's Life is relationship: the ecstatic interaction
between the Father, Son, and Spirit that makes them three distinct Persons while remaining indivisibly One. So the key to our
Life as Christians is commitment to *relationship*: relationship
with God, relationship with other human persons, and on another level, relationship with all that God has made.

Jesus taught that in our interaction with other persons, our
first concern should be to preserve and foster relationship with
them. That is our first priority.

The three examples Jesus gives show how we should respond
when our relationship with others is threatened by concern about
our property, our time, or by feelings of rejection. They all show
overwhelming Kindness and Generosity.

Property. If the disagreement is over property, Jesus says, "If
anyone wants to take your coat, give your cloak as well." In other
words, Christians should never break off their relationship with
anyone because of concern about money or possessions. Rather
than lose the relationship, we should give others whatever they
want. More than that, we should be generous and give them even
more than they ask. This is Patient Endurance expressed in an act
of Kindness extended into unexpected Generosity: "give your
cloak as well."

A word of caution, however: this principle only applies to maintaining relationships that are authentic. Sometimes just giving in would amount to acceptance of a totally false relationship. Then it is called "enabling."

Time. If the problem is that someone is making unjustified, even unreasonable, demands on our time, Jesus says: "If anyone forces you to go one mile, go also the second mile."

Roman soldiers had the right to require any citizen of an occupied country to guide them one mile along their way. Jesus says that if an enemy soldier takes us out of our home or shop to guide him for one mile, we should go with him two miles instead—just to say that good relationship—even with a foreign soldier—is worth more to us than our time.

That applies even more to people we live and work with who, by not doing their job as they should, make our job harder or longer. It applies to everyone who imposes on our time. We should not only endure them; we should respond with Kindness and Generosity to show that we value our relationship with them more than we value our time. (Again, we repeat the warning against enabling.) This is more than Patient Endurance; it is Patient Endurance expressed in acts of Kindness extended into unexpected Generosity: "go the second mile."

Rejection. Those challenges are slight compared to the third one. If we offer our hand to someone in friendship and receive in return a rejection that is like a slap in the face, Jesus says to offer our hand—to stick out our neck—a second time. "If anyone strikes you on the right cheek, turn the other also." Risk another rejection. We should keep making ourselves vulnerable as long as there is any hope of forming a good relationship.

This is more than human patience or endurance. It is more than ordinary kindness. It is a desire for, and a commitment to, *relationship* that takes us to the length of love displayed by Jesus on the cross.

> For the grace of God has appeared, bringing salvation to all....For we ourselves were once foolish, disobedient, led astray, slaves to various passions and pleasures, passing our days in malice and envy, despicable, hating one another. But when the goodness and loving kindness [*chrestotes kai philanthropia*; literally, "kindness and love for humankind"] of God our Savior appeared, he saved us, not because of any works of righteousness that we had done, but according to his mercy, through the water of rebirth and renewal by the Holy Spirit. ▪ TITUS 2:11; 3:3-5

This fruit of the Spirit appeared in the Patient Endurance of Jesus (or "passionate endurance," since "patience" and "passion" come from the same root), expressed in the loving Kindness and Generosity he showed in his act of dying on the cross. He did that in order to enjoy with every one of us the overwhelming gift of relationship that is the Life of the Father, Son, and Spirit. And no matter how much or how often we keep rejecting Jesus through the evil we do, he keeps responding with Kindness and Generosity. He keeps turning "the other cheek."

In every Mass we celebrate the unbelievable Kindness and Generosity that is Jesus's response today to what we did to him in his passion: "He took bread and gave it to his disciples, saying, 'Take this, and eat it. This is my body.'"

This is what Jesus says to us, and does for us every time he gives himself to us in Communion. That is Kindness. That is Generosity. That is awesome.

The same fruit of the Spirit appears in us, and is "poured out on us richly through Jesus Christ our Savior"(Titus 3:6), when we go to the lengths of love to maintain our divine relationship with every human being on earth. Then we are the "aroma of Christ" in the world.

BEYOND HUMAN GOODNESS

All the examples given above seem impossible. If the whole human race did what Jesus teaches here, there would never be another war. No families would be divided over arguments about inheritance. Broken friendships would be rare. More marriages would survive.

What Jesus is saying here is that we should value relationship with others over every other value on earth. Why? Because God does. God's Life is relationship: three Persons interacting with each other in Love.

Ah, but for God that is easy! All three Persons are perfect. Of course they love each other! But how can we on earth give first priority in our lives to relationship with people who are dishonest and disagreeable, who don't respect us or our rights, who even do us violence?

Jesus began his list of examples above with the radical—"root"—principle: "Do not resist an evildoer." He concludes with:

> "You have heard that it was said, 'You shall love your neighbor and hate your enemy.' But I say to you, love your enemies and pray for those who persecute you, so that you may be children of your Father in heaven; for he makes his sun rise on the evil and on the good, and sends rain on the righteous and on the unrighteous." • MATTHEW 5:43–45

That is Patient Endurance. That is Kindness. That is Generosity.

The key to the New Law of Jesus, the guiding truth we need to keep in mind when reading anything he says, is that Jesus is not teaching us how to be good human beings; he is teaching us how to live as children of our Father, who "makes his sun rise on the evil and on the good, and sends rain on the righteous and on the unrighteous."

The "Grace of the Lord Jesus Christ" has made us divine. We are to live and love on the level of God. "I give you a new commandment, that you love one another *just as I have loved you*" (John 13:34).

The scriptural description of God dealing with human persons is "enduring love." Those are the words Moses heard when God promised, "I will make all my goodness pass before you, and will proclaim before you my name" (Exodus 34:19). And the phrase appears seventy times more in Scripture.

> God's love has been poured into our hearts through the
> Holy Spirit that has been given to us. For while we were
> still weak, Christ died for the ungodly....For a good person
> someone might actually dare to die. But God proves the
> love of God for us in this: that while we still were sinners
> Christ died for us. ▪ ROMANS 5:5–8

Patient Endurance, Kindness, and Generosity are the fruit of Love "poured into our hearts through the Holy Spirit." They are the fruit of the Spirit, the "aroma of Christ," the "fragrance that comes from knowing him," evidence that we are children of the Father.

> "If you love those who love you, what credit is that to you?
> For even sinners love those who love them. If you do good
> to those who do good to you, what credit is that to you?
> For even sinners do the same. If you lend to those from
> whom you hope to receive, what credit is that to you? Even
> sinners lend to sinners, to receive as much again.
>
> "But love your enemies, do good, and lend, expecting
> nothing in return. Your reward will be great, and you will
> be children of the Most High; for he is kind to the ungrate-

ful and the wicked. Be merciful, just as your Father is
merciful." ▪ LUKE 6:32-36

When the word for the Kindness that is a fruit of the Spirit is used
about God in Scripture, it is almost always used in contrast to
severity. God is kind to everyone, but above all to those who do
not deserve it.

"God is kind to the ungrateful and the wicked." ▪ LUKE 6:35

Do you despise the riches of God's kindness and forbear-
ance and patience? ... God's kindness is meant to lead you
to repentance. ▪ ROMANS 2:4

God, who is rich in mercy ... loved us even when we were
dead ... so that ... God might show ... God's ... kindness
toward us in Christ Jesus. ▪ EPHESIANS 2:4-7

That gives Kindness a natural connection to Patience. "Love is
patient; love is kind ..." (1 Corinthians 13:4).

But showing patience out of kindness to those who don't
deserve it requires generosity. So the fruits of Patience, Kindness,
and Generosity are inseparable.

The word we translate as "generosity" is *agathourgeo*, from
agathos, "good," and *ergon*, "to do." Generosity is the characteristic of someone who wants to do good. But for Christians, this is
not ordinary human generosity. That is clear from the story of the
young man who asked Jesus what he must "do" to inherit eternal
life (Mark 10:17–27):

As he was setting out on a journey, a man ran up and knelt
before him, and asked him, "Good Teacher, what must I do
to inherit eternal life?"

Since the man said "eternal" life, which is exclusively the Life of God, instead of "everlasting life," which could be just the prolongation of human living, Jesus noted the switch in dimensions and applied it to the difference between human good and transcendent (divine) Good:

> Jesus said to him, "Why do you call me good? No one is Good but God alone."

He was preparing the man to see that Jesus is not just a teacher of life that is good, but the unique Teacher of Life that is Good, Life on the level of God.

Before the man could reply, Jesus gave a preliminary answer to his question restricted to the level of doing ordinary human "good":

> "You know the commandments: 'You shall not murder. You shall not commit adultery. You shall not steal. You shall not bear false witness. You shall not defraud. Honor your father and mother.'"

But the man was looking for more. He was generous. He wanted to do more than the "good" the commandments called for.

> He said to him, "Teacher, I have kept all these since my youth."

Then Jesus invited him to do the Good that is divine:

> Jesus, looking at him, loved him and said, "You lack one thing; go, sell what you own, and give the money to the poor, and you will have treasure in heaven; then come, follow me."

Jesus was inviting him to make a dramatic gesture of generosity that would show he accepted divine Life, Life on the level of God. To show that he was ready to "dream the impossible dream" and do what is impossible to humans but is made possible to those who share in God's divine Life by "the Grace of the Lord Jesus Christ."

But the man turned him down. He had generosity, but not the Generosity that is the fruit of the Holy Spirit.

> When he heard this, he was shocked and went away grieving, for he had many possessions. Then Jesus looked around and said to his disciples, "How hard it will be for those who have wealth to enter the kingdom of God!" The disciples were perplexed at these words. But Jesus said to them again, "Children, how hard it is to enter the kingdom of God! It is easier for a camel to go through the eye of a needle than for someone who is rich to enter the kingdom of God." They were greatly astounded and said to one another, "Then who can be saved?" Jesus looked at them and said, "For mortals it is impossible, but not for God; for God all things are possible."

The "fruits of the Spirit" are just that: they are not the fruits of living an ordinary human life. They are the aura of Grace, the "aroma of Christ," the "fragrance that comes from knowing him" with the divine knowledge of Faith and loving him and others in a way that is only possible for those who are living the divine Life of his body on earth.

That is how we should strive to present ourselves to others, especially when they treat us badly. If others see us showing this overwhelming Patience, Kindness, and Generosity, our lives will proclaim the Good News.

HOW DO WE DO THIS?

If we are going to be the "aroma of Christ" in the world, and to all around us, we need to bring all this down to ground level and put it to the test of our daily experience. So let's do that:

- Do I see that the key to Patient Endurance is responding with positive acts of Kindness to annoyances, insults, or injustices?
- Do I cultivate "an abiding inclination to be of assistance" in action?
- Do I get up in the morning to spend my day being kind to others?
- Throughout the day, do I keep my focus on what I can do for others, instead on what others are doing to me, or not doing for me?
- When anyone wrongs me, imposes on me, or annoys me in any way, is my immediate reaction to "be of assistance" by doing something kind? And generous?
- Is my first priority in life relationship? Cultivating relationship with God and other human persons?
- Do I refuse to break off my relationship with anyone because of a concern about money or possessions? Rather than lose (an authentic) relationship, do I prefer to give to others whatever they want—even more than they ask? Do I do it with Kindness and unexpected Generosity?
- When people I live and work with make my job harder or longer by not doing the things they should, do I respond with a Kindness and Generosity that show I value relationship with them more than my time?
- If I offer someone friendship and receive a rejection that is like a slap in the face, am I willing to stick out my neck again and risk another rejection? Will I keep making myself vulnerable as long as there is any hope of forming or maintaining a good relationship?

- Does the Passionate Endurance of Jesus on the cross, powered by his loving Kindness and Generosity, inspire me to "go to the lengths of love" to form or maintain with every human being on earth the relationship that is the Life of the Father, Son, and Holy Spirit?
- What reasons can I offer for giving priority to relationship with people who are dishonest, disagreeable, or even do us violence?
- Do I accept that Jesus is not teaching us how to be good human beings but how to be Good children of our Father? What is the difference between divine and human goodness when it comes to Patient Endurance, Kindness, and Generosity?
- Do I agree that the divine Kindness that is a fruit of the Spirit is kindness to everyone, but above all to those who do not deserve it?
- What do I think would be the effect on the world if a significant number of Christians spread the "aroma of Christ" around them through the Patient Endurance, Kindness, and Generosity described here?
- Do I understand Pope Francis's warning: "Being patient does not mean letting ourselves be constantly mistreated, tolerating physical aggression or allowing other people to use us"? Do I have enough self-confidence (or trust in the Spirit's guidance) not to confuse Patience and Kindness with enabling?

The Aroma of
FAITHFULNESS

*I was overjoyed when some of the friends arrived
and testified to your faithfulness to the truth,
namely how you walk in the truth.*   3 JOHN 3

The seventh fruit of the Spirit is Faithfulness.

Through Faithfulness God "spreads in every place the fragrance" that comes from living our religion in a way that radiates the truth of our *relationship* with God.

The aura that surrounds Christians should be the aroma of a covenanted people. Christians have something to be faithful to, like the married who wear a ring. And we have the assurance that God will be faithful to us.

Our religion is a religion of relationship. It is not a religion of rules, any more than marriage is defined by rules.

Because of this, Faithfulness is the fruit of the Spirit that most explicitly reveals our acceptance of God the Holy Spirit. It is through the Holy Spirit that we experience our relationship with the Father and the Son.

> It is that very Spirit bearing witness with our spirit that we are children of God.…And because we are children, God has sent the Spirit of his Son into our hearts, crying, "Abba! Father!" ▪ ROMANS 8:16; GALATIANS 4:6

It is only through the Holy Spirit that we can know Jesus as the Son.

> No one can say "Jesus is Lord" except by the Holy Spirit.
> ■ 1 CORINTHIANS 12:3

And we experience our graced (divine) relationship with one another in the "communion of the Holy Spirit," the "common union" of being guided by the Spirit within us all.

> The Grace of the Lord Jesus Christ, the love of God [the
> Father], and the communion of the Holy Spirit be with all
> of you. ■ 2 CORINTHIANS 13:13

In the *epiclesis* during the Eucharistic Prayer at Mass we pray that we may be "gathered into One by the Holy Spirit."

Paul fought all his life against those who, instead of faithfulness in following the Spirit, wanted to make Christian identity consist in obedience to rules.

> You foolish Galatians! Who has bewitched you?...Did
> you receive the Spirit by doing the works of the law or by
> believing what you heard? Are you so foolish? Having start-
> ed with the Spirit, are you now ending with the flesh? Did
> you experience so much for nothing?...Does God supply
> you with the Spirit and work miracles among you by your
> doing the works of the law, or by your believing what you
> heard? ■ GALATIANS 3:1–5

That is the choice: to focus on rules or focus on relationship. Faithfulness, as the fruit of the Spirit, makes it evident that all of our dealings with God and others are based on consciousness of a covenanted relationship, "communion in the Holy Spirit." That relationship belongs to the essence of Christianity.

HOW DO WE DO THIS?

If we are going to be the "aroma of Christ" in the world, and to all around us, we need to bring all this down to ground level and put it to the test of daily experience. So let's do it:

- Do I live my religion in a way that radiates Faithfulness to the relationship I have with God as Father? With Jesus as friend and Savior, sharing my body with me? With the Holy Spirit as Counselor and guide? With other people as co-believers, co-laborers to establish the reign of God on earth?
- What in my life makes it visibly evident that my religion is a religion of relationship rather than a religion of rules?
- When I examine my conscience, do I ask what rules I have broken, or whether I have been faithful to a covenanted relationship with God and others?
- Do the people who know me think of me as "moral," or as faithful to a deeply felt relationship with God? Why?
- When I refuse to do something wrong, do I say it is because God forbids it, or because "I wouldn't do that to God"?
- What concrete actions or choices in my life show that my religion is a religion that seeks relationship with God, and others? What do I do just to know God better?
- Do I understand that I am related to all Christians as members of Christ's body, and that we are all "sons and daughters in the Son?" How does this awareness motivate me to interact with others?
- Do I believe I can actually be "friends" with the infinite, transcendent God who is Being Itself? What makes that kind of relationship with God possible? Am I doing what it takes?
- What in my life makes manifest the fruit of the Holy Spirit that is Faithfulness? Does it proclaim the Good News?

The Aroma of
GENTLENESS

"Come to me, all you that are weary and are carrying heavy burdens, and I will give you rest. Take my yoke upon you, and learn from me; for I am gentle and humble in heart, and you will find rest for your souls." MATTHEW 11:28–29

The eighth fruit of the Spirit is Gentleness.

The Greek word Paul uses for Gentleness is *prautes*. Aristotle (*On Virtues and Vices*) described it as "tranquility and stability of spirit, the virtue of not being easily provoked to anger." Jesus used it to describe himself as "gentle and humble in heart." And Paul told his converts he was "gentle among you, like a nurse tenderly caring for her own children" (Matthew 11:29; 1 Thessalonians 2:7). When Paul had to address division among the Corinthians he said he preferred to come, not with the power of "a stick," but with the power of "love, in a spirit of gentleness."

Wherever Christians walk and talk, the "aroma of Christ" that surrounds them should make everyone around them conscious of the Good News that our God is a gentle God, a God of mercy and compassion, who sent Jesus, not to intimidate, but to inspire; not to drive people through force, but to lead them through persuasion and attraction.

Jesus taught us to call God "Father," in preference to (although not to the exclusion of) "Lord," and to focus on the kind of gentle love and care God has for us as Father.

Jesus's own relationship to the Father was the key to his Gentleness in his relationships with others:

> "As the Father has loved me, so I have loved you....
> Everyone the Father gives me will come to me, and anyone
> who comes to me I will never drive away." ▪ JOHN 6:37; 15:9

> "Take care that you do not despise one of these little ones;
> for, I tell you, in heaven their angels continually see the face
> of my Father in heaven." ▪ MATTHEW 18:10

His ministry to others was for him an experience of union with the Father:

> "I know my own and my own know me, just as the Father
> knows me and I know the Father. And I lay down my life
> for the sheep....Know and understand that the Father is in
> me and I am in the Father....The Father and I are one."
> ▪ JOHN 10:14, 30

> Jesus, knowing that the Father had given all things into his
> hands, and that he had come from God and was going to
> God...got up from the table...and began to wash the disci-
> ples' feet. ▪ JOHN 13:3–5

Isaiah described Jesus as the embodiment of the Father's Gentleness:

> Here is my servant, whom I have chosen, my beloved, with
> whom my soul is well pleased. I will put my Spirit upon
> him, and he will proclaim justice to the Gentiles. He will
> not wrangle or cry aloud, nor will anyone hear his voice in
> the streets. He will not break a bruised reed or quench a

smoldering wick until he brings justice to victory. And in his name the Gentiles will hope. ▪ MATTHEW 12:18–21

The reality of Christian Gentleness is that it is the total relinquishment of all power to God. Jesus let himself be killed because he refused to count on any power except the power the Father chose to use. When Peter wanted to defend him, he said, "Put your sword back into its sheath. Am I not to drink the cup that the Father has given me?...Do you think that I cannot appeal to my Father, and he will at once send me more than twelve legions of angels?" (John 18:11; Matthew 26:53).

> "I lay down my life in order to take it up again. No one takes it from me, but I lay it down of my own accord. I have power to lay it down, and I have power to take it up again. I have received this command from my Father."
> ▪ JOHN 10:17–18

It was in this same spirit of reliance on the Father that he sent out his apostles: "Peace be with you. As the Father has sent me, so I send you" (John 20:21).

And he sent the Holy Spirit into our hearts so that we would know the Father's Gentleness from within:

> For we did not receive a spirit of slavery to fall back into fear, but rather a spirit of adoption. When we cry, "Abba! Father!" it is that very Spirit bearing witness with our spirit that we are children of God. ▪ ROMANS 8:15–16

> And because we are children, God has sent the Spirit of his Son into our hearts, crying, "Abba! Father!" So we are no longer slaves but children; and if children then also heirs.
> ▪ GALATIANS 4:6–7

So Christians should always proclaim—not only in word and action, but by their attitude, their "aura," their way of dealing with people—the Good News that our God is a gentle God. We are sent out into the world to be "the aroma of Christ," who "through us spreads in every place the fragrance that comes from knowing him" (2 Corinthians 2:14).

The "fragrance that comes from knowing him" is the fruit of the Holy Spirit known as Gentleness.

GENTLENESS IS A STUMBLING BLOCK

But Gentleness is not always acceptable. What shocked people most in Jesus as Messiah, and should shock people today in Christians as his body on earth, is the renunciation of power.

What at first won people to Jesus during his earthly life—although it was not what he wanted—were his "deeds of power," his healing miracles (see, for example, Matthew 11:21, 13:54; Luke 19:37). People thought he was going be the kind of messiah they expected: an earthly king who would use divine power to make them victorious over their enemies and give them an enjoyable, satisfying life in this world.

But Jesus knew he was not sent to be that kind of messiah. After he had fed five thousand people in the desert and "the people saw the sign that he had done," he "realized that they were about to come and take him by force to make him king." So he "withdrew" up the mountain to escape them (John 6:15).

His "deeds of power" (healing miracles) inspired the crowds to throng enthusiastically into Jerusalem with him on the day we celebrate in liturgy as "Palm Sunday":

> The whole multitude of the disciples began to praise God
> joyfully with a loud voice for all the deeds of power that
> they had seen, saying, "Blessed is the king who comes in

the name of the Lord! Peace in heaven, and glory in the
highest heaven!" ▪ LUKE 19:37

But Jesus knew he was entering Jerusalem to die. The only power
Jesus would rely on was power compatible with Gentleness: the
power of truth and love. The hope Jesus gives us is based on trust
in the Father, who chooses to act through Gentleness.

When Pilate asked him, "Are you the King of the Jews?" Jesus
answered, "My kingdom is not of this world. If my kingdom were
of this world, my followers would be fighting to keep me from
being handed over to the Jews. But as it is, my kingdom is not
from here."

"So you are a king?"

"You say that I am a king. For this I was born, and for this I
came into the world, to testify to the truth. Everyone who belongs
to the truth listens to my voice" (John 18:33–37).

That is the way of Gentleness.

When Jesus was on trial before the Sanhedrin, what actually
got him sentenced to death was the absence of power. In the context it was seen as a proof of blasphemy:

> The high priest asked him, "Are you the Messiah, the Son of
> the Blessed One?"
>
> Jesus said, "I am; and 'you will see the Son of Man
> seated at the right hand of the Power,' and 'coming with the
> clouds of heaven.'"
>
> Then the high priest tore his clothes and said, "Why
> do we still need witnesses? You have heard his blasphemy!
> What is your decision?" All of them condemned him as
> deserving death. ▪ MARK 14:61–64

In the context, claiming to be Messiah after God had let him be
handed over to his enemies meant Jesus was claiming to be God.

There was no sign of divine power protecting him. According to Scripture as it was understood at that time, this proved Jesus could not be the Messiah. Scripture said, "By this I know that you are pleased with me; because my enemy has not triumphed over me" (Psalm 41:11). A messiah without the backing of God's power was a contradiction in terms.

So when Jesus, in spite of his powerlessness, still claimed to be the Messiah, he was saying that he needed no divine affirmation. Being Messiah was his identity, not just a call from God. He was the Messiah by nature. To say this amounted to saying he was God.

That is when the high priest tore his garments in sign of blasphemy and declared him deserving of death.

The Gentleness of Jesus, his refusal to use power, is what made some people also turn against him. They had put their hopes in Jesus to save them from the Romans. But when Pilate brought him out to them—bound, tortured, and obviously abandoned by God—and declared sarcastically, "Here is your King!" all their hope turned to disappointment, their disappointment turned to rage, and they cried out: "Away with him! Away with him! Crucify him!"

Pilate asked them, "Shall I crucify your King?" The chief priests answered, "We have no king but Caesar" (John 19:14–15). They chose power over Gentleness. As a nation, so do we.

Later, under the cross, the people "stood by, watching," while the leaders "scoffed at him, saying, 'He saved others; let him save himself if he is the Messiah of God, God's chosen one!'"

Even the soldiers mocked him: "If you are the King of the Jews, save yourself!" And one of the criminals crucified with him kept deriding him: "Are you not the Messiah? Save yourself and us!" (Luke 23:35–37).

It was Jesus's renunciation of power that turned everyone against him. They just could not understand how anyone could

"save" them without using force to deliver them from their enemies. That was why they rejected Jesus as Messiah. And it may
be the reason why we still do today—whether we admit it or not.

In the measure that we, as a nation, reject the way of Gentleness
in favor of force, violence, and power, we reject the way of Jesus.
And we reject Jesus himself.

THE CHALLENGE OF NONVIOLENCE

The most obvious way we do this, of course, is by rejecting nonviolence. Even if we argue against total nonviolence, insisting
on some right of self-defense, it is clear that as a nation we are
far from Christian in the way we use and approve of force, even
deadly force.

Not only do we engage in wars that do not meet the criteria of
the traditional "just war theory," but our manner of waging war
cannot be defended. Our stockpiling of nuclear weapons speaks
for itself about American rejection of Vatican II's vehement
declaration:

> Any act of war aimed indiscriminately at the destruction
> of entire cities or extensive areas along with their popula-
> tion is a crime against God and humanity itself. It deserves
> unequivocal and unhesitating condemnation.
>
> ▪ *CONSTITUTION ON THE CHURCH IN THE MODERN WORLD*, 80

That is why the fruit of the Holy Spirit known as Gentleness does
not appear in us as a nation. We are not a Christian nation.

In his 2017 World Day of Peace Message, *Nonviolence: A Style
of Politics for Peace*, Francis said:

> To be true followers of Jesus today also includes embrac-
> ing his teaching about nonviolence....In the world there is
> too much violence, too much injustice, and...this situation

cannot be overcome except by countering it with more love, with more goodness. This *"more"* comes from God…

For Christians, nonviolence is not merely tactical behavior but a person's way of being, the attitude of one who is so convinced of God's love and power that he or she is not afraid to tackle evil with the weapons of love and truth alone. Love of one's enemy constitutes the nucleus of the "Christian revolution." The Gospel command to love your enemies (cf. Luke 6:27) is rightly considered the *magna carta* of Christian nonviolence. It does not consist in succumbing to evil… but in responding to evil with good (cf. Romans 12:17-21), and thereby breaking the chain of injustice.

Francis had said in his address to new Vatican ambassadors on December 15, 2016:

Nonviolence is a typical example of a universal value that finds fulfilment in the Gospel of Christ but is also a part of other noble and ancient spiritual traditions. In a world like our own, sadly marked by wars and numerous conflicts, to say nothing of widespread violence evident in various ways in day-to-day life, the choice of nonviolence as a style of life is increasingly demanded in the exercise of respon-sibility at every level, from family education, to social and civil commitment, to political activity and international relations. In every situation, this means rejecting violence as a method for resolving conflicts and dealing with them instead through dialogue and negotiation.…

This is not the same as weakness or passivity; rather it presupposes firmness, courage and the ability to face issues and conflicts with intellectual honesty, truly seeking the common good over and above all partisan interest.…Some peoples, and indeed entire nations, thanks to the efforts of nonviolent leaders, peacefully achieved the goals of freedom and justice. This is the path to pursue now and in the future. This is the way of peace—not a peace proclaimed by words but in fact denied by pursuing strategies of domination, backed up by scandalous outlays for arms, while so many people lack the very necessities of life.

Francis was even more explicit in his published interviews with Dominique Wolton in *Politique et Société*:

> Today we need to rethink the concept of a "just war." We have learned, in political philosophy, that, to defend ourselves, one can make war and consider it just. But can we define any war as "just"? Or as a "defensive war"? The only just thing is peace….I do not like to use the term "just war." We hear, "I make war because I have no other means to defend myself." But no war is just. The only just thing is peace.

America may be filled with Christians, but we are not a Christian nation. It says something good about us that we put "In God we trust" on our currency, but our budget makes it obvious that our real trust is not in God but in military force and economic power.

As the Church, we must stand up against this element of American culture if we want to be the "aroma of Christ" in the world.

In the United States, we still put the children of our Father to death violently if they are found guilty of murder, whether they are repentant or not. We criticize some politicians for keeping it legal to inflict violent death on unborn babies in the womb; and we criticize others for keeping it legal for all Americans to possess guns that let them inflict violent death on everyone else. But the truth is, we are all to blame for accepting what Pope John Paul II, in his 1995 encyclical *The Gospel of Life*, called the "culture of death."

THE ILLUSION OF POWER

The root of the problem is our addiction to power—not just to military and physical power but to economic power, corporate power, hierarchical and clerical power, the power of personal position and prestige. We use power constantly in the way we speak to each other, exercise authority, and push to get things done.

When persuasion doesn't work, we use power to get things done. We choose force over Gentleness. Anytime we shout at others to get things done, we lose the fruit of Gentleness.

If a child asks, "Why do I have to do this?" and a parent answers, "Because I said so," that is a denial of the faith! The correct answer is, "Because God says so. I have to tell you what to do because I have to obey God. I am 'responsible,' which means I have to 'answer' to God for what I let you do. Jesus said, 'If you love me, you will obey my commands' (John 14:15). So if you love me, you will obey mine."

Any act of governing others that is not at the same time obedience to God is an abuse of power.

The truth is that Jesus rejected every use of power except the power of truth and love. He came to invite and to persuade, not to intimidate or control. That is the way of Gentleness. If his words seem threatening at times, it is only because he is telling us the truth about threats that already exist. When a doctor says, "Stop smoking or you will die," that is not intimidation; it is mercy. It is the same when Jesus tells us where our way of life is leading us.

Saint Paul spoke like Jesus when he wrote to Philemon (1:8–9), "Though I am bold enough in Christ to command you to do your duty, yet I would rather appeal to you on the basis of love—and I, Paul, do this as an old man, and now also as a prisoner of Christ Jesus." Paul showed the fruit of Gentleness.

Jesus doesn't seem to have reacted with anger against anyone but the Pharisees. Against them he spoke, not only with anger but with rage. In Matthew's chapter 23 he is furious. But to the woman taken in adultery he was gentle; as he was with the Samaritan woman who had had five husbands and currently was not married to the man she was living with (John 4:17; 8:10).

He "reproached" the cities that, even after he worked miracles for them, "did not repent." But his final words were:

> "Come to me, all you who are weary and are carrying heavy burdens, and I will give you rest. Take my yoke upon you, and learn from me; for I am gentle and humble in heart, and you will find rest for your souls. For my yoke is easy, and my burden is light." ▪ MATTHEW 11:28–30

He showed the same gentle spirit toward Jerusalem:

> Jerusalem, Jerusalem, the city that kills the prophets and stones those who are sent to it! How often have I desired to gather your children together as a hen gathers her brood under her wings and you were not willing! ▪ MATTHEW 23:37

Even when the people of his hometown wanted to hurl him off a cliff, Luke tells us Jesus just "passed through the midst of them and went on his way" (Luke 4:30).

PROACTIVE GENTLENESS

The gentle are not passive. They "resist evil with love." They resist, however, not with destructive violence, but through constructive criticism and constructive action designed to bring about change.

This is to resist with the strong Gentleness that is the fruit of the Holy Spirit in our hearts. We must insist—gently but firmly—on *dialogue*, on what Francis calls "a synodal Church."

A synodal Church is a listening Church. And we must be aware that listening is more than just hearing. It is a reciprocal listening in which each one has something to learn.

Let us never forget this! For the disciples of Jesus, yesterday, today and always, the only authority is the authority of service, the only power is the power of the cross. In the words of the Master: "You know that the rulers of the nations lord it over them, and their leaders oppress them. It shall not be so among you: but whoever wants to become great among you must be your servant, and whoever wishes to be first among you must be your slave" (Matthew 20:25–27). "It shall not be so among you": in this expression we touch the heart of the mystery of the Church and receive the necessary light to understand hierarchical service.

▪ *CATHNEWS, NEW ZEALAND, OCTOBER 20TH, 2015*

This is the fruit of Gentleness. Francis is calling for a Church in which decisions are arrived at through dialogue and discernment. This calls for the renunciation of power—not of authority, because authority is necessary in the Church, but of authority exercised from "on high," unilaterally, or "autocratically" (from the Greek *autos* "self" and *kratos* "power"). For Christians, power never comes from one's self alone, and is never exercised for one's self alone.

As a fruit of the Holy Spirit, the blessing of Gentleness is that it reinforces *relationship*. A Christian always acts out of relationship with God as Father, Son, and Spirit, conscious of relationship with others, and for the sake of relationship with others. A mother is gentle with her child because of their relationship. Doctors are gentle with their patients, and employers with their employees, when there is a sense of relationship. We are harsh only when we treat other people as objects. If we act in partnership with Jesus, conscious that he is acting *with us* and *in us* and *through us*, we cannot be anything but gentle. We are yoked to him who said: "Take my yoke upon you, and learn from me; for I am gentle and humble of heart" (Matthew 11:29).

If Christians turn away from power, renouncing it from the heart, our lives will be characterized by the fruit of the Spirit that is Gentleness. And our Gentleness will envelop us in the "aroma of Christ," the "fragrance of the knowledge of God."

Then we will proclaim the Good News.

"Let your Gentleness be known to everyone. The Lord is near" (Philippians 4:5).

HOW DO WE DO THIS?

If we are going to be the "aroma of Christ" in the world, and to all around us, we need to bring all this down to ground level and put it to the test of our daily experience. So let's begin:

- Would those who know me best say I am "gentle and humble of heart"? What do I do that would make them say it or not say it?
- Does my attitude, my "aura," my way of dealing with people, proclaim the Good News that our God is a gentle God?
- Do I think that what shocks people today in Christians is our renunciation of power? What examples can I give that support my opinion?
- Do I see people today being drawn to God or to Jesus today by his "deeds of power"—for example, by his answers to their prayers? Do others turn away from religion when their prayers don't appear to be answered? What do people seem to expect from religion?
- Have I ever seen people turn away from God because of God's refusal to use power in the world, in the Church, or just for themselves as they think God should? What do people hope Jesus will save them from?

- Do I believe that in the measure we reject the way of Gentleness in favor of force, violence, and power, we actually reject Jesus?
- What is my stance toward nonviolence?
- Do I see a lack of Gentleness in the way Christians use:
  - » military and physical power?
  - » economic power?
  - » corporate power?
  - » hierarchical and clerical power?
  - » the power of personal position and prestige?
- Do I use power frequently in the way I speak to others, exercise authority, push to get things done? Do I recognize this as sin?
- When persuasion doesn't work, do I use power? Choose force over Gentleness?
- If my child asks, "Why do I have to do this?" do I ever answer, "Because I said so!"? How should I answer?
- In my exercise of authority, is it evident to everyone that I am only doing what I have to do? That I am obeying God?
- Do I "resist evil with love"?—through constructive criticism and constructive action designed to bring about change? Or am I just passive?
- Do I insist on—and am I willing to take part in—dialogue and discernment about decisions to be made in my parish and diocese?
- Do I experience the blessing of Gentleness as reinforcing my *relationship* with God and others?

The Aroma of
SELF-CONTROL

*You must make every effort to support your faith with goodness...
knowledge... self-control... endurance... godliness... mutual affection,
and... love. For... they keep you from being ineffective and unfruitful
in the knowledge of our Lord Jesus Christ.* 2 PETER 1:5–8

The ninth fruit of the Spirit is Self-Control.

"Self-control" suggests the natural virtue of being in control of oneself, the strength of self-mastery, domination of one's "lower" passions by the higher powers of intellect and will.

It is this, of course. But as a fruit of the Holy Spirit, Self-Control cannot be something simply natural. And, in fact, its true reality is surrender.

The "self" being controlled is not our "lower" self, our body and our passions, but our whole self: everything we are. If one's whole self is being controlled, it must be by someone other than one's self. That someone is God. The fruit of the Holy Spirit's action in us is *surrender*:

- surrender to the Spirit, by whom we are called to live (see Romans 8:5; Galatians 5:25);
- surrender to Jesus, as the members of a body are to their head (see Colossians 1:18);
- and "in Christ," surrender to the Father, because Jesus is surrendered to the Father

> Then comes the end, when Jesus hands over the kingdom
> to God the Father….For he must reign until he has put all
> his enemies under his feet….When all things are subject-
> ed to him, then the Son himself will also be subjected to
> the one who put all things in subjection under him, so that
> God may be all in all. ▪ 1 CORINTHIANS 15:24–28

Because, as a fruit of the Holy Spirit, Self-Control is the total surrender of our humanity to God, it is the fruit of the Spirit that
most explicitly reveals our *"knowledge of our Lord Jesus Christ"* as
God the Son in the mystery of his self-emptying to be "found in
human form."

> Let the same mind be in you that was in Christ Jesus, who,
> though he was in the form of God, did not regard equal-
> ity with God as something to be exploited, but emptied
> himself, taking the form of a slave, being born in human
> likeness. And being found in human form, he humbled
> himself and became obedient to the point of death—even
> death on a cross. Therefore God also highly exalted him
> and gave him the name that is above every name, so that at
> the name of Jesus every knee should bend, in heaven and
> on earth and under the earth, and every tongue should
> confess that Jesus Christ is Lord, to the glory of God the
> Father. ▪ PHILIPPIANS 2:5–11

When Jesus "emptied himself, taking the form of a slave, being
born in human likeness," he gave up during his lifetime the exercise of divine control over the world, over the people in it, and
even over what would be done to his own body. He became
obedient—surrendered—to the point of death—even death
on a cross.

This is the key to the incarnation.

In Jesus, God the Son "humbled himself." And all who want to "let the same mind be in them that was in Christ Jesus" must give up all disordered attachment to maintaining control through wealth, prestige, and power over their own lives, the lives of others, and over human events. The fruit of the Spirit that is Self-Control is the "aroma of Christ" that surrounds those who accept—and understand—the mystery of the incarnate Son of God. His was the divine Self-Control of surrendering all control into the hands of the Father. There is no control of self—of one's whole self—that is more complete, more life-giving, or more in contradiction to the thinking of this world than this. But for those who are able to perceive it, it is the "aroma of Christ," the "fragrance of the knowledge of God."

In particular, it is the "aroma of victory," the "fragrance of the triumph" of Jesus over all the powers of this world. When those who have the mind of Christ see Jesus today, in the human body of his Church, "emptying himself, taking the form of a slave," then they know that God has "exalted him and given him the name that is above every name, so that at the name of Jesus every knee should bend, in heaven and on earth and under the earth, and every tongue should confess that Jesus Christ is Lord, to the glory of God the Father."

This is self-evident to those who have "the mind of Christ." But not everyone does, even in the Church. What many, both clergy and laity, want is a Church that projects the image of control, because in the mindset of this world, when everything seems to be under control, that gives the illusion of power, security, and success.

Francis pleads against insistence on an "orderly" and "perfect" Church in which everything is "just right"—*comme il faut*—when he writes in *The Joy of the Gospel*, 49:

> Let us go forth, then, let us go forth to offer everyone the
> life of Jesus Christ....I do not want a Church....caught up

in a web of obsessions and procedures. If something should rightly disturb us and trouble our consciences, it is the fact that so many of our brothers and sisters are living without the strength, light and consolation born of friendship with Jesus Christ, without a community of faith to support them, without meaning and a goal in life. More than by fear of going astray, my hope is that we will be moved by the fear of remaining shut up within structures which give us a false sense of security, within rules which make us harsh judges, within habits which make us feel safe, while at our door people are starving and Jesus does not tire of saying to us: "Give them something to eat" (Mark 6:37).

Francis gives some characteristics of those who have the "mind of this world":

> Spiritual worldliness, which hides behind the appearance of piety and even love for the Church, consists in seeking not the Lord's glory but human glory and personal well-being. It is what the Lord reprimanded the Pharisees for: "How can you believe, who receive glory from one another and do not seek the glory that comes from the only God?" (John 5:44)....
>
> This insidious worldliness is evident in a number of attitudes....In some people we see an ostentatious preoccupation for the liturgy, for doctrine and for the Church's prestige, but without any concern that the Gospel have a real impact on God's faithful people and the concrete needs of the present time. In this way, the life of the Church turns into a museum piece or something which is the property of a select few....
>
> It can also lead to a business mentality, caught up with management, statistics, plans and evaluations whose principal beneficiary is not God's people but the Church as an institution.

> [In all of these] the mark of Christ—incarnate, cru-
> cified and risen—is not present. Closed and elite groups
> are formed, and no effort is made to go forth and seek out
> those who are distant or the immense multitudes who
> thirst for Christ. Evangelical fervor is replaced by the empty
> pleasure of complacency and self-indulgence.
>
> ▪ *JOY OF THE GOSPEL*, 93–95

Behind, underneath, and throughout all of these false attitudes
is a basic dependence on control. And all of them fall under the
heading of *triumphalism*, the third of the three viruses the bishops
rejected—along with *legalism* and *clericalism*—in the first session
of the Second Vatican Council as deep resources of corruption in
the Church.

What is triumphalism?

Triumphalism is the exact opposite of the Self-Control through
surrender that is a fruit of the Spirit. Triumphalism is an infection
in the Christian spirit that thinks the victory of Christ is made
visible by being expressed and celebrated in the language of this
world. It is a perversity that seeks security and status in worldly
signs of success embodied in the Church. For triumphalists, the
glory of God is shining out on earth through the riches, prestige,
and power of God's Church. The Church is rich; the Church is
respected. Whenever we gather together we see signs of order
and control. Everyone's role is clearly defined. And everyone is
following protocol. The authorities are clearly in charge. There
are rules, and they are being obeyed. No one seems disturbed.
Everything says we are a successful Church. This is the proof and
the assurance that, if we just keep doing what we are doing, we
will be doing everything God expects us to do.

Most likely, if any sins are condemned from the pulpit, they will
be sins that go against the human self-control of the orderly life
that everyone expects in a Church that conforms to the cultural

values of the "right kind of people." The focus is often on issues to which most of those in our middle-aged congregations are hardly tempted, like abortion and same-sex marriages. But condemning them confirms us in our righteousness. No one is made to feel guilty for the unexamined enjoyment of affluence and prestige, for a culturally conformist lifestyle, or for exclusively profit-focused business practices. Or for not following the teachings of the Sermon on the Mount. Or for not reading Scripture as a disciple of Jesus Christ. Or for not bearing witness as a "prophet" by living a lifestyle that raises eyebrows because it embodies the shocking values of the gospel. Or for not ministering as a "priest in the Priest" all day, every day, by giving physical expression to faith, hope, and love in every encounter with another person. Or for not taking responsibility as a "steward of the kingship of Christ" for bringing about changes that transform society. In a Church that projects the image of wealth, prestige, and orderliness we feel assured that everything is "under control" and as it should be. There is nothing to disturb our complacency or encourage our restlessness for more.

This image of control is a perversion of the Self-Control that is the fruit of the Holy Spirit. The fruit of the Spirit is surrender to letting God be in control. When what we see in the Church assures us that everything is under control, this should warn us everything is out of control. Humans have wrenched the steering wheel out of the hands of the Spirit, and the Church is careening toward disaster.

The fruit of the Spirit that is Self-Control appears in the Church when it is obvious that each one of us—and the Church as a community—believes that nothing is under control unless we are surrendered to God. Usually the sign of that is a visible absence of attachment to wealth, prestige, and power.

Paul wrote:

> If I must boast, I will boast of the things that show my
> weakness....The Lord said to me, "My grace is sufficient for
> you, for power is made perfect in weakness." So, I will boast
> all the more gladly of my weaknesses, so that the power
> of Christ may dwell in me. Therefore I am content with
> weaknesses, insults, hardships, persecutions, and calamities
> for the sake of Christ; for whenever I am weak, then I am
> strong. ▪ 2 CORINTHIANS 11:30; 4:9–10

When it is obvious in the Church that humans are not pretending to be in control, then we are surrounded by the aura of that Self-Control that is the fruit of the Spirit. That is the aroma of the incarnate Christ, the fragrance of the knowledge of the mind of God.

Then we will proclaim with credibility the Good News.

HOW DO WE DO THIS?

If we are going to be the "aroma of Christ" in the world, and to all around us, we need to bring all this down to ground level and put it to the test of our daily experience.

So let's do it:

- How does the refusal to "run a tight ship" reveal acceptance of God the Son in the mystery of his self-emptying, "taking the form of a slave"? When do I consciously imitate Jesus in that?
- In my life, how do I try to exercise control over myself? over others? over things I am involved in?
- In each of my answers to the question above, when is my control surrender to God, and when is it just self-assertion?
- Does the way I live my faith give me a sense of security based on my behavior? Does it make me feel superior to others when I "observe certain rules or remain intransigently faithful to a particular Christian style from the past"?

- What kind of religious services do I like best—those in an impressive church, in which all at the altar are wearing beautiful vestments, the choir is singing beautiful music, and all the ceremonies are dignified and stately; or those in a simple chapel, with inexpensive vestments and furnishings, in which the people are singing hymns that they know, and the presiding minister is very informal, making eye contact with the people, and trying to draw everyone into the action?
- If I like both ways of worshiping, what does each way "say" to me? What image of the Church do I see in each one? Which shows more "concern that the gospel have a real impact on God's faithful people and the concrete needs of the present time"?
- Did the way Jesus dressed and dealt with ordinary people distance him from them or invite familiarity? Does the way I speak and act with clergy and bishops encourage them to follow the self-emptying of Jesus? If not, is there anything I should change?
- Where do I see evidence that people in the Church think the victory of Christ is made visible by being expressed and celebrated in the status symbols of this world? Does it give me a sense of security and importance when I see worldly signs of success embodied in the Church?
- How can I make the Self-Control of surrender to God that is the fruit of the Spirit so visible in my life and the life of the Church in the modern world that it *keeps me from "being ineffective and unfruitful in the knowledge of our Lord Jesus Christ,"* and lets me spread the "aroma, the fragrance of the knowledge" of God the Son made flesh to be like one of us?

Make a Beginning

S top. Don't just read about the gifts and fruits of the Spirit. Use them.

Use the gift of Understanding to be sure you understand what you have read. Use the gifts of Knowledge and Counsel to help you figure out how to make practical use of what you understand. Use the gift of Wisdom to keep yourself focused on your reason for living, on God's reason for giving you existence, and on the full promise of life.

Use the gift of Family Spirit to sweeten your relationship with every human being. And use the gifts of Strength and Awe of the Lord when you need extra motivation to move yourself forward or hold yourself back.

Don't live by the gift and powers of human nature alone. Live by the gifts of the Spirit. They empower you to live the Life of God.

If you use the prayer "Come, Holy Spirit" that opens this book, you ask every day that you *may not be conformed to this world, but transformed by the renewal of your mind,* so that you might discern and do *what is good, and acceptable* (or pleasing) *to God, and perfect* (Romans 12:2). You are declaring that your heart's desire is not just to do what is "good" by avoiding sin. Nor is it just to do what is "acceptable" and "pleasing" to God in someone called to bear witness by manifestly living the divine life of God as a Christian. You are asking to do what is "perfect" by living in total surrender to "Christ in you, the hope of glory" (Colossians 1:27).

This means to "live by the Spirit" and "be guided by the Spirit" (Galatians 5:25).

To see whether you are living the Life of God or not, check to see whether the fruit of the Spirit is visible in your life. By your fruit you will know what you are (see Matthew 7:16; Luke 6:43).

Let this book be a new beginning for you. Live "life to the full." Live on the level of God.

And the peace of God, which surpasses

all understanding, will guard your hearts

and your minds in Christ Jesus.

PHILIPPIANS 4:7

NOTE

This book is based on the *Doctrine Spirituelle* of the French Jesuit Louis Lallemant (1588–1635), written during the 1620s, published in French in 1694, and finally translated into English in 1855 by Frederick W. Faber. The *Doctrine Spirituelle* is a collection of conferences and exhortations Lallemant gave when he was "tertian instructor," i.e. spiritual formator of Jesuits who spent their final stage of formation under his guidance. Among those were Saints Isaac Jogues and John Lalande, who, along with Saint René Goupil and five other Jesuits, were killed in Canada by the Mohawks and canonized in 1930 as the North American Martyrs.

A modern translation of the *Doctrine Spirituelle*, by Patricia M. Ranum, Chestnut Hill, MA, is available through the Institute of Jesuit Sources, 2016, 357 pages. Or search *The Spiritual Doctrine of Father Louis Lallemant of the Company of Jesus*, Malvern Classics, Kindle Edition, © copyright 2013 Beth Maynard.

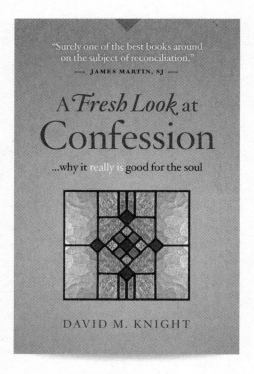